From earlier times to the Jacobite risings, clans answered the call of their chiefs. In more modern times, the call has been to the British armed forces and, notably, the famous Highland regiments, such as the Gordon Highlanders.

The two World Wars called for a much larger scale of mobilisation, involving civilians as well as those who served in the armed forces.

Local resident Fiona Hunter became intrigued by the names of men listed on the Braemar war memorial from World War I and began to research them and their stories. She then combined forces with Maureen Kelly, a keen historian and writer, and her husband, Tom Kelly, who were, at the same time, doing similar research on the names from both World Wars and also chronicling some of the many facets of Braemar's involvement.

Many local residents, as well as others from further afield, too numerous to mention, have contributed memories and reminiscences and even some amusing anecdotes which have helped to bring the research to life. To them we extend our heartfelt gratitude.

The result is this fascinating booklet which tells the stories of the local men who died in the two wars and of local activities to support the war effort. It also reminds us of the course of war in the two largest conflicts of the 20th century.

There have been many unexpected discoveries. During WWII, Braemar's challenging mountains and harsh climate provided an ideal training ground for Britain's special forces. Tom Kelly was astonished to learn that his father had trained for mountain warfare in Braemar with commandos under the leadership of the famed mountaineer John Hunt. We hope you will find connections of your own to Braemar in wartime.

For further information on BLHG and its activities please visit our website at
www.braemarlhg.com

© Braemar Local History Group. November 2020 Edition Two

Published by Tandemkelly. ISBN 978-1 8382192-0-8

WARTIME BRAEMAR

ACKNOWLEDGEMENTS

- Air Training Corps
- Canadian Forestry Corps
- Commando Veterans Archive & Ray Brooks
- Gordon Barclay
- Greg Young, 15th Battalion CEF Memorial Project
- Joe Dorward
- The Gordon Highlanders Museum, Aberdeen
- The Imperial War Museum
- The National Army Museum
- Peter Lyon Nicol & Braemar Buzzard
- RAF Pathfinders Archive
- Richard E Flaff, UK Airfields Archive
- Society of Antiquaries of Scotland
- WW2Talk Archive

WARTIME BRAEMAR - INTRODUCTION

It is sometimes hard to believe today that for nine years during the first half of the 20th century so much of the developed world was involved in major armed conflict.

The war of 1914-18 is remembered as either the 'Great War' or 'World War I' because of its unprecedented intensity and its spread from Europe to the oceans and continents elsewhere. It was also the first major war fought in the air as well as on land and at sea.

The scale of fighting, casualties, and destruction on the Western Front and Eastern Front in Europe, and mobilisation of civil populations, were unprecedented. Naval conflict extended throughout the Atlantic, and other campaigns were fought in the Balkans and north east Mediterranean, across Africa and the Middle East, and the Asian rim of the Pacific. By the time the war was over it is thought that more than 16 million people – soldiers and civilians – were dead.

The Second World War of 1939-45 was the inevitable but delayed consequence of military expansion and invasions of neutral countries in the late 1930s by Germany in Europe, by Italy in Africa, and by Japan in the Far East and Pacific.

Britain and France tried to delay another war in Europe by diplomatic means which came to an abrupt end when Germany invaded Poland in 1939. The USA tried to curb Japanese expansion by economic embargoes (particularly on oil supplies) until Japan attacked Pearl Harbor, without declaration of war, in December 1941. From that point it was all-out warfare on land, at sea and in the air between the Axis countries – Germany, Italy , and Japan – and the Allies – USA, Britain and its Empire, and Russia after it was invaded by Germany in August 1941.

Braemar community, along with communities the length and breadth of the country, paid a heavy toll in servicemen in both World Wars. The purpose of Part 2 of this booklet is to remember the losses and to understand a little about the men's lives and experiences. For this reason, their personal details have been accompanied with an account of the theatre of war in which they were serving.

During both wars, the community 'back home' in Braemar played a significant supporting role not only in such activities as fundraising but also in hosting different war-related groups. Part 1 of the booklet describes some of these activities.

PART 1 - BRAEMAR IN WARTIME

BRAEMAR IN WWI
(items in italics from newspapers of the day)

RECRUITMENT

Britain declared war on Germany on 4 August 1914, the very day German forces invaded neutral Belgium. Three days later, Lord Kitchener, Secretary of State for War, called for volunteers to enlist in the armed forces. Meetings to encourage recruitment were held throughout the UK. A very large number, including *many ladies* attended a meeting in Braemar on 3 September at which Mr Farquharson of Invercauld and various Clergy urged *the manhood of Braemar to come forward to assist in this just war* stressing that although the mission of the Church was to preach a gospel of peace, they could, at this time, *best serve peace by advocating war.* Many men, supported by their friends and womenfolk, volunteered.

In May of the following year, a further step was taken when Parish Councils were required to carry out a census of *men of authorised military age.* This provided lists for conscription which was introduced in January 1916, initially for single men then later also for married men.

RELIEF FUNDS FOR SOLDIERS AND SAILORS

From early in the war, various funds collected money to provide relief for the armed services. Newspapers reported on donations to such funds from the people of Braemar, for example, as early as August 1914 St Margaret's Episcopal Church Needlework Guild gave £32 to the Prince of Wales National Relief Fund and a few months later gave £17 to the Red Cross.

In September 1914 a scheme to sew garments was set up in Braemar by Princess Dolgorouki – a very wealthy Edwardian Socialite, married to a Russian Prince, who had rented Braemar Castle since 1897 and who, during her visits, became much involved in village activities. She organised a war garment work party in Braemar Castle, providing not only wool and flannel for the village ladies to sew but also tea and cakes to encourage them in their labours! The Princess took the finished garments with her to London for the Lady Mayoress's appeal for clothing for wounded soldiers and sailors.

Soon other schemes were introduced to provide cigarettes and knitted items of clothing such as mitts, mufflers and socks for the servicemen. Over the coming months the Braemar Parish Church Woman's Guild and other groups sent parcels of garments to Lord Robert's Fund for Indian Troops, to the 1/7th Gordon Highlanders' Comforts Fund – the fund set up to supply 'comforts' to the local regiment in which many Braemar men served – and to Captain Hayward in Aberdeen for the navy.

RELIEF FOR BELGIAN REFUGEES

Early in WWI, 250,000 refugees, around 95% of whom were Belgians, fled to the UK. The Daily Telegraph established a *Shilling Fund for the Relief of Belgians* and, again, Princess Dolgorouki took the lead in Braemar arranging for the collection of shillings. Braemar responded generously and by October 1914 had donated *889½ shillings* (£44 9s 6d, now £44.47p). Aid for Belgian refugees did not stop there. The Braemar YWCA also undertook *noble work . . . by preparing warm garments for little refugee Belgian boys and girls* as did the Braemar Parish Church Guild.

In Autumn 1914, Mrs Macdonald, Manageress of the Fife Arms Hotel, took in four wounded Belgian soldiers who were nursed back to health as guests of the hotel. Although conversation was almost impossible because of language difficulties, their appearance on arrival had indicated times of great hardship. Prior to their re-joining their regiment in January 1915, they took up the invitation of Princess Dolgorouki to visit Braemar Castle. Their only recorded comment was that *its walls were thicker than the walls of Belgian Fortresses.* Perhaps the December cold of an unoccupied castle (Princess Dolgorouki having long since returned to London), chilled their enthusiasm!

1ST SCOTTISH GENERAL HOSPITAL

The 1st Scottish Territorial Force General Hospital in Aberdeen (often called 1st Scottish General Hospital) was one of four military hospitals in Scotland during WWI which catered for war wounded. Each of these hospitals had a number of affiliated hospitals providing additional beds and/or specialist treatment. Given the strains on Government funding and with no National Health Service, hospitals had to rely quite heavily on donations of money and goods. The administration of the donations was the responsibility of the Red Cross.

Concert at 1st Scottish General Hospital, Aberdeen

Wartime newspapers regularly carried detailed reports of donations for the 1st

Scottish General Hospital in Aberdeen. Braemar not only provided money but also knitted 'comforts', flannel bed shirts and food. Included among the food contributions from Braemar were 2½ brace of grouse and 25 rabbits. Mrs Macdonald of the Fife Arms Hotel gave flowers and rhubarb – no doubt providing both comfort and relief! The children of Braemar Public School carried out a fortnightly collection of eggs from villagers as part of the National Egg Collection *for our wounded Tommies*. The number collected varied but at one good *laying time* reached 92 eggs. The eggs were forwarded by the headmaster to the Red Cross depot in Aberdeen – hopefully arriving intact!

BRAEMAR WAR WORK ASSOCIATION

As time passed, War Work Associations or Work Parties were set up throughout the land to co-ordinate fund-raising and other war support activities in towns and villages. Braemar's very active War Work Association, established in January 1916, was affiliated to the national body and in due course received certificates of recognition and badges from the War Office.

The Braemar War Work Association took over the organising of monetary collections such as the 'penny-a-week' collection for the Red Cross, fund-raising concerts, whist drives, sales of work and garment knitting. Monthly newspaper reports detailed the amounts raised and numbers of garments forwarded to Headquarters in Aberdeen. Most reports were very satisfactory but on one occasion the report indicated that fewer items were being knitted at present as the members were *busy otherwise*! No explanation of *otherwise* was given!

SPHAGNUM MOSS

Treatment of wounds of so many thousands of casualties in the fighting led to acute shortages of dressings. With no antibiotics, prevention of sepsis was a huge challenge. But very early in the war, botanist Isaac Bayley Balfour and surgeon Charles Cathcart, both from Edinburgh University, found a solution. When cleaned and dried, sphagnum moss had antiseptic properties and could hold 22 times its weight in liquid (which was twice as absorptive as cotton). So, the cry went up for people to collect the sphagnum moss known to thrive in the peaty, cold, damp areas of the Scottish Highlands.

Sphagnum Moss in Braemar

Braemar War Work Association took up the challenge knowing that sphagnum moss was abundant on the hillsides around the village. Men, women, children and even visitors joined forces to gather the moss into large bags. The bags were then sent to the Edinburgh collection centre for cleaning and drying before being packed into muslin bags which were used for dressing battlefield wounds. Collection of the moss normally started in late May/early June and continued till the winter weather set in. A newspaper in early November 1916 congratulated Braemar on collecting over 420 bags of moss that year and indicated that the Braemar War Work Association hoped to reach 500 bags before the snows and frosts stopped collection.

ZEPPELIN OVER DEESIDE

With one exception, all the war action was far from Braemar. On 2 May 1916, however, a raid by eight Zeppelins (massive German airships) set out to attack the Forth Bridge and the British fleet at Rosyth and Invergordon, and to cause civilian panic and unrest by terror bombing. Fortunately for Scotland, the weather that night was appalling. Zeppelin L20 got lost. Confusing the Rivers Forth and Tay and thinking that the eastern Grampians were the Fife coalfields, the crew dropped a bomb there, causing little more damage than an injured horse and some broken windows.

Blinded by the rain and mist, L20's wayward journey continued up Deeside and Glen Lui. Realising he was completely lost, the Zeppelin Commander dropped a 'water flare' hoping it would show him to be over the sea! Great was the surprise and fear of the McDonald family below in their remote and lonely highland cottage, Luibeg, at the southern entrance to the Lairig Ghru pass, to hear the sound of airship engines. "It made an afa queer noise a Zeppelin – zoom, zoom" said the daughter, Nell.

By this time running low on fuel, the commander of L20 had no option but to turn east towards home. L20 got as far as crash landing in Norway where many of the crew were interned for the remainder of the war, although the Captain managed to escape seven months later and make his way back to Germany.

Some five years after that eventful night, Nell's father, Sandy, found an object buried in the heather and wondered what it was and if it would explode. Edward, The Prince of Wales, with whom Sandy was stalking a couple of days later, was fascinated by the find. He took it to the Air Ministry for identification. They reported that it was the nose-cone of the Zeppelin water flare. The Prince returned the nose-cone to Sandy with a note: 'Sandy McDonald from Edward P. It's quite safe now!' The cone remained in the family's possession for many years and is now in the Grampian Transport Museum, Alford.

German Zeppelin Airship

THANKSGIVING FOR WAR'S ENDING

On Tuesday 12 November1918, the day after the armistice which ended WWI, Braemar held a joint service of thanksgiving in the then Parish Church (now flats opposite The Invercauld Arms Hotel). The Aberdeen Press & Journal of Wednesday 13 November carried the following report:

The Princess Royal at Braemar Thanksgiving

A joint thanksgiving service was held in Braemar Parish Church yesterday. The Rev Alexander Saunders gave a suitable address. The congregation included HRH the Princess Royal and the Princess Maud, and the household from Mar Lodge. A few ladies and gentlemen gifted a handsome sum of money for sweets, which were distributed to the scholars.

BRAEMAR IN WWII

World War II was declared on 3 September 1939. As in WWI, considerable effort was given in Braemar to raising recruits, money and goods for the war effort. Collection of sphagnum moss for wound dressing was resumed but to a lesser extent than for the previous war. There were also several new activities which had a major impact on village life, including the arrival of groups coming to Braemar for various war-related reasons.

BELGIAN SCHOOL IN THE INVERCAULD ARMS HOTEL 1941 - 1945
(information source – 'Memories of Braemar 1941-45' by Belgian pupils and teachers, edited by Mary Hunter)

When the Germans invaded Belgium in May 1940, many families and children fled to Britain. They were housed in different parts of London and elsewhere. As the Blitz intensified, the Belgian Government in exile decided to establish rural boarding schools for over 2000 Belgian refugee children, well away from any bombing. One site chosen was The Invercauld Arms

Belgian Pupils and Teachers at Invercauld Arms Hotel

Hotel, Braemar. Thus, in October 1941, around 100 Belgian children between the ages of 12 and 18, along with some Belgian teachers, arrived in Braemar, many staying until the end of the war.

Despite having to cope with new surroundings and, for many, being separated from family and friends for the first time, the children settled remarkably quickly into the strict discipline regime of their new school. A number did, however, find local customs such as 'no football on a Sunday' somewhat disappointing! They soon found other activities, however, and enthusiastically joined the Braemar Companies of the Belgian

Soup queue at the Belgian School

Guides in Great Britain and the Belgian Scouts in Great Britain which were established for them by local Guide and Scout leaders. A Braemar Belgian Flight of Air Training Cadets was later established for older Belgian and Braemar boys. In all these groups, the Belgian children mixed with other branches throughout Aberdeenshire.

Their regular Sunday attendance at St Andrew's Church, Braemar was a considerable boost to the local Roman Catholic congregation as was their music teacher who sometimes played the organ at the services. Great was the entertainment of the children when they managed to persuade him to play a well-known, melodic Belgian folk song during the service. Happily, the local congregation were unaware of its rather risqué words!

The very cold hard winters were a new experience for most of the children. They loved the sledging but had mixed feelings about one particular snow fall which was so bad that they were able to touch the snow from their windows on the first floor. The village was cut off for some days and they ran out of fresh milk. The breakdown of their electricity was quite fun not least because it enabled them to get up to all sorts of mischief in the resulting darkness!

In one piece of well-remembered mischief, a few boys climbed out their bedroom window and down a drainpipe one dark night, wandered around the village and, finding clothes hanging on a washing line, removed a pair of gents' long drawers (ie underpants) and 'flew' them from the highest flagpole in the Princess Park (now the Princess Royal & Duke of Fife Memorial Park). Outrage was the village response next morning when the drawers were spotted. Happily for the culprits, the Canadian woodsmen (see later section), with their reputation for heavy drinking, got the blame!

Belgian Guides with their flag

The Belgian boys loved football and especially enjoyed the times when they could play a game against soldiers staying at the Fife Arms Hotel for mountain training (see later section). In order to make some money before they left Braemar at the end of their training, some of these soldiers sold their possessions (including even their weapons). Several of the Belgian boys thereafter were able to sport a Commando dagger and at least one 'innocent' banjo case was found to contain – not a banjo, but a revolver!

The Invercauld Arms Hotel was a great site for the school. Not only was it a large building but it had extensive attics among the roof rafters, mainly used for storage. One night, curiosity got the better of a boy who spotted a trap door in the roof of the small toilet cubicle he was using. By standing on the edge of the toilet bowl he managed to open the trap door and hoist himself into the space above. All was dark, dusty and full of menace. When a flash of light suddenly appeared in the distance, he scrambled back through the trap door, heart pounding.

That escapade was, however, the start of midnight adventures for a group of the boys. Armed with torches and balls of string (so that they could find their way back) they explored this dusty 'Aladdin's cave' – full of antlered deer heads, stuffed eagles, tartan adornments, piles of crockery, heaps of outdated magazines, 'mysterious' boxes, disused mattresses and other discarded items. One janitor, who reported hearing ghosts moving above him in the night was treated with derision by other staff members. The adventures finally ended one night, however, when a new member of staff became suspicious at the length of time a boy (whose turn it was to be on guard) was spending in the toilet. When the boy was eventually persuaded to unlock the door, he stepped out of the tiny cubicle clutching an obscure text in Arabic, only to be followed by 'a veritable platoon of scantily dressed boys'!

The time came, after the war was won, for the children to return to Belgium. Their feelings were very mixed on that day in July 1945 when they left Braemar – their beautiful, safe home of four years which had brought them such fun, friends, a Scots accent and so very many happy memories.

Mar Lodge Canadian Lumber Camp
Canadian Forestry Corps

CANADIAN LUMBER CAMP: MARCH 1942 - JUNE 1944
(with thanks to the Canadian Forestry Corps and also to Joe Dorward for permission to use their information)

In both WWI and WWII, British demand for wood increased greatly. To meet the war needs, it was estimated that five trees required to be felled for every soldier. This resulted in a wood supply crisis as Britain had previously imported most of its wood. With recruitment to the armed forces, there was no spare British labour to increase felling of home-produced timber. In WWII, as in WWI, the solution came from Canada where, in 1940, a unit of woodsmen, the Canadian Forestry Corps (CFC) was created within the Canadian Army. After military training, companies from the CFC were sent to different parts of Scotland to harvest the large forests. Thus, on 30 March 1942, around 200 Canadian woodsmen, belonging to No 25 Company, arrived in Braemar and set up a lumber camp in the Mar Estate on the north side of the River Dee at its junction with the River Lui.

Their initial job was to build the camp and the sawmill as well as to construct roads, a light railway and a wooden bridge across the River Dee. In addition, they installed a water-powered electricity generator. The accommodation huts were wooden, each housing 14 men. There were also several Nissan huts which not only housed armourers, carpenters etc but which, with their semi-circular corrugated iron shape, were excellent bomb shelters. In addition, the woodsmen constructed a 'big ditch' or pond with water intake from the River Lui. This enabled the huge tree logs to be floated and manoeuvred more easily into the sawmill mechanism as well as removing some dirt acquired on the journey from the hillside. After the war it was used as a swimming pool by the young of Braemar!

The woodsmen worked in two sections – one cutting down the timber with handsaws and axes and transporting it to the sawmill, and the other sawing it into 'lumber' in the sawmill and loading it onto the light railway for transport over the bridge to the waiting trucks. The relative openness of the Scottish forests (rather than the Canadian tangled undergrowth) was welcomed by the woodsmen but the alternating rain and snow which made timber very wet and difficult to handle, was not! The short winter days which limited possible working hours were also an inconvenience. On a Saturday they were required to undertake additional military training which could be target practice or, on occasions, a joint exercise with some of the Mountain Warfare Training units (see next section).

Braemar villagers were fascinated by the modern, sophisticated logging and transportation equipment brought over by the Canadians as well as by the electricity generator. They much appreciated the straightening of the Linn O'Dee road carried out by the Canadians to ease and speed the wood transport to Ballater station. Assistance from the woodsmen on days of very heavy snow was also very welcome. On such days, the Canadians would feed the starving deer and, with their bulldozer snow ploughs, help to clear some of the streets around Braemar. One oft-repeated story tells of a Canadian bulldozer driver receiving hospitality in a Banchory pub after clearing Banchory streets of snow. It was not until the thaw arrived that he was found also to have 'cleared' the street of kerbstones!

Narrow gauge railway hauling lumber over the Canadian Dee bridge. Its demolition in 1962 after storm damage was mourned by locals and hikers.
Joe Dorward - CC BY.SA 4.0

Life in the Canadian camp was not all work. The woodsmen swam in the River Lui and, in season, dammed the River Lui to trap salmon. In their battle dress with its distinctive cap badge, they were easily recognised in the village attending church or playing in their pipe band. Their contribution and kindness to the children at Christmas and other festive occasions plus their football games with the Belgian school lads were very much appreciated and valued by the community, particularly as so many of the children's fathers were away in service. The woodsmen's presence at dances and entertainments in the village was also extremely popular . . . especially with the ladies!

Mar Lodge 'big ditch' pond
Joe Dorward - CC BY.SA 4.0

MOUNTAIN WARFARE TRAINING FROM THE FIFE ARMS HOTEL 1942 - 1945

After the disastrous attempt by the Allies to assist the Norwegians to resist the German invasion of Norway in 1940 and the subsequent successful operations by Free Norwegian Commando units, the British decided they required an elite fighting force which would be effective in extreme winter mountain conditions. In December 1942, they established the Commando Snow and Mountain Warfare Training Camp (CSMWTC) in Braemar. The Cairngorms with their remoteness, loneliness, treacherous crags and snow-filled gullies provided an ideal training ground for the extreme conditions the Commandos might have to face in a sustained operation in Norway or other European mountain areas. The Headquarters of the CSMWTC was established in the requisitioned Fife Arms Hotel. Its first Commanding Officer was Squadron Leader Frank Smythe, an accomplished Everest mountaineer. Second in Command and Chief Instructor, was Major John Hunt, (later Sir John Hunt who led the 1953 successful ascent of Mount Everest).

Commandos attending the courses lived, not in the luxury of the hotel, but in 2-man tents in Glen Clunie (near the site of the current caravan park). They were provided with clothing suited to mountain conditions. Instead of greatcoats and tightly knitted woollens, they wore loose string vests under angora shirts, long drawers with seamless legs, wind-proof smocks and trousers, peaked caps with ear flaps, cold weather boots, gloves and goggles. In addition, CO Frank Smythe told the Alpine Club in December 1945, the camp was well *'stocked with Greenland sledges, ski and snow shoes. There was even talk of recruiting a dog team from the local canine populace which ranged from Alsatians to Pomeranians; it would have provided a noble spectacle.'* There was one problem, however: very little snow that winter!

Three full Commando units, 1, 4 and 12 were, nevertheless, trained at Braemar from December 1942 until around the end of May 1943 when it was decided that the Commandos should transfer to Wales for more specific training in rock climbing. In their place, in June 1943, came the Lovat Scouts, who had been chosen to become the Mountain Recce (Reconnaissance) Regiment for the 52nd Division. They were ideally suited to mountain training being mainly hardy highlanders with a deer-stalking and ghillie background. Again, only the headquarters was in the hotel with the Lovat Scouts living in a tented camp in Glen Clunie near

Commandos on mountain exercise, Braemar

Glen Clunie Lodge. During the summer, the Lovat Scouts also undertook the role of Guards to the Royal Family at Balmoral. By the end of their Braemar training in October 1943, when the Regiment moved to Snowdonia to be trained in rock-climbing by the Commando School, their Glen Clunie tented camp was apparently a sea of mud. After the Lovat Scouts came units from the 52nd Lowland Division, but amusingly known as the 'Mountain Division'.

Courses at the Braemar Mountain Warfare Training Camp lasted six weeks. Training was intense but was graded to make sure in the early stages never to test a man beyond his limit. During the last two weeks, however, trainees were presented with a series of very strenuous tactical exercises aimed to include as many as possible of the lessons and skills learned over the preceding weeks. The trainee, carrying a 70lb pack of food and equipment (including weapons and ammunition) on his back, was often required to climb several high tops and spend a few days in the Arctic conditions, sometimes living in dug out snow holes and surviving on pemmican – a mixture of dried meat, fat and dried berries. On other occasions they were required to camp overnight before climbing crags such as Mitre Ridge on Beinn a' Bhuird with its treacherous rocks and crumbling overhangs.

Commandos resting during training in Braemar. Major John Hunt reclining at rear; middle row left (with pipe) Bill Kelly (Tom's Dad)
Ray Brooks & Commando Veterans Archive

Mule Team

To assist trainees on long marches by transporting their heavy equipment and weapons over mountain areas impossible for wheeled vehicles, pack mules from the Indian Mule Company, along with turbaned Indian troops to handle them, were brought to Braemar. One trainee, Joe Brown, writing of a long gruelling march through the Lairig Ghru pass, praised the surefootedness of the mules over even the roughest track or climb. He also well remembered, when very broken ground was reached, having to man-handle the mules' heavy equipment over the boulders before reloading it onto the backs of the mules for the next part of the journey.

The arrival of the Indian mules caused much stir among the Braemar inhabitants. Villagers who were children at the time, remember

Indian Army Mule Team, Braemar
Joe Brown, WW2Talk website

sitting on a wall, hearing the 'clip clop' and then watching the mules being led into the village ready for their part in one of the major exercises. The mules, along with the Camp's pack horses, were held in a field in Glen Clunie belonging to Balnellan farm (now Braemar Caravan Park). Complaints from villagers of unacceptable noise, however, led to the mules having to be moved to a field at Glen Clunie Lodge some miles along the road towards the Cairnwell!

Gun Practice

Other memories of the Mountain Warfare Training in Braemar are still shared among the older members of the community. Mortar bomb practice took place at the top of Chapel Brae near the pond. A launching platform was set up from which the mortar bombs were fired over the Dee. Each shell was counted and its point of contact logged. Bombs which did not explode had to be recovered for detonation elsewhere. To facilitate access to the unexploded bombs, a temporary tree trunk bridge was constructed over the river Dee. Until it was demolished a few years after the war, the tree bridge proved a fun crossing point for youngsters.

The river Clunie behind the camp headquarters in the Fife Arms Hotel was used for hand-gun target practice at balloons floating on the water. Other attractions for locals, especially kids, were test firing of the big guns and a joyride on a bren gun carrier from its parking place behind the building which is now Gordon's Restaurant.

There was also fascination with the parachute flares fired high into the air from Creag Choinnich. The small parachutes descending, with their flares below lighting up the area, were a magical sight. Acquiring one of the fallen parachutes was also desirable as they provided enough silk to make a small petticoat or a pair of silk knickers!

Fun and Games

Not all military life was geared towards war training, however. Not only were there football games with boys from the Belgian School in the Invercauld Arms Hotel but, on one occasion, a gymkhana was held on Braemar golf course with officers riding the horses and competing over high jumps and slaloms. Suddenly, Bill Geddes, an Argentinian who was teaching the trainees how to load and handle the pack mules and horses, came riding bareback into the gymkhana on a mule with only a rope for a rein. Without difficulty, he and the mule (which he called 'Diabolo' – the Devil) cleared all the jumps and wove through the slalom . . . much to the entertainment of the onlookers!

AIRCREW MEMORIAL 1939-1945

Over the years, many aircraft have crashed in the mountains around Braemar, particularly so during WWII when military aircraft were flying over the area, sometimes in poor visibility.

In 2003, a monument was created in the centre of Braemar next to the War Memorial in memory of the aircrew of one particular aircraft, a Vickers Wellington bomber, R1646, which had crashed in January 1942. The Monument also commemorated all other WWII aircrew who had lost their lives in the Cairngorm mountains. The Memorial was unveiled on 21 August 2003 by HRH, Princess Anne, The Princess Royal. During the ceremony, wreaths were laid by representatives of the Air Forces of Britain, Canada, Australia and New Zealand and flowers were laid on behalf of relatives of the Wellington bomber aircrew. The ceremony finished with a flypast by a Tornado aircraft from RAF Lossiemouth.

Vickers Wellington Bomber R1646 – crashed 19 January 1942

The winter of 1941-42 was one of the worst for many years in Braemar with very heavy snow falls and low temperatures. On 19 January 1942, a Vickers Wellington bomber, R1646, with eight crew left the NE Scotland airbase at RAF Lossiemouth on a training flight. When the plane did not return it was listed as missing, most likely over the North Sea. The plane had, in fact, crashed into a Cairngorm hillside and lay undiscovered in the snow.

Some weeks later the Wellington wreckage was spotted by a gamekeeper from the Invercauld Estate and a young lad from Braemar. It was sticking out of deep snow in a narrow corrie in Upper Glen Clunie just north of the summit of Carn Aosda, quite close to the main A93 road to Braemar. A search party set out and, after clearing a path through the deep snow and cutting steps in the ice below, managed to reach the wreckage. Over the next two months the bodies of the crew were recovered and buried in Dyce Old Churchyard (near RAF Dyce, now Aberdeen Airport). The aircraft wreckage, other than valuable parts, was left on the mountain. Some Braemar young folk, who visited the wreckage shortly after its discovery, fashioned a few rings from a section of metal windscreen surround. At least one of those youngsters remembers wearing her ring for many years in memory of the aircrew who had died.

Sixty years later, Andy Brown, whose visit to the site as a youngster in 1942 had left lasting memories, obtained permission from the Ministry of Defence to recover the engines from the aircraft and use one as the centre of the memorial in Braemar to the Wellington bomber aircrew and all other WWII aircrew who died in the Cairngorm mountains.

Airspeed Oxford PH 40 04 – crashed 10 January 1945

On 10 January 1945, an RAF Airspeed Oxford, PH40 04, with a crew of five members of 311 (Czech) Squadron RAF set off from RAF Tain on the North East Coast of Scotland, bound for RAF Hornchurch, near London. The aircraft was taking Flying Officer Jan Vella to London to receive a decoration at Buckingham Palace. The other four crew were going on a short leave. The aircraft never arrived and, as no crashes had been reported, was assumed lost over the sea.

This Is To Commemorate
The Supreme Sacrifice
Made By Those Aircrew Of
The Royal Air Force
And Their Allies Of World War II
And In Subsequent Years Who Were
Killed Flying In These Mountains

Placed On This Site
On 18th September 2005 By Cadets
And Staff From Aberdeen
And NE Scotland Wing ATC
Aided By The Royal British Legion
And The MacRobert Trust

It was not until seven months later that the wreckage and bodies were discovered by two men hill walking on Beinn a' Bhuird. Because of the inaccessibility of the site, it took 10 days and the assistance of Indian Army mules based in the Mountain Warfare Training School in Braemar, to remove the bodies which were taken for burial in the Brookwood Military Cemetery, near Woking in Surrey.

Sixty years later, in 2005, it was agreed that the Air Training Corps (ATC) should place a granite inscribed plaque at the site of the crash as part of their Duke of Edinburgh award programme. Like the Aircrew Memorial in the village, it was again in memory, not only of that aircrew, but of all other military aircrew who had been killed flying in the Cairngorms during WWII and the following years. A helicopter conveyed representatives to the site for a ceremony of dedication on Sunday 18 September 2005 which was followed by a short service conducted by Rev James Wood, Wing Commander and Minister of the ATC, at the Braemar War and Aircrew Memorials in the centre of the village.

During work on the memorial site on Beinn a' Bhuird, a watch was found with, engraved on the reverse, the name of the pilot of the crashed plane. The watch was taken for cleaning and repair and, in the company of the ATC, was presented to the pilot's family at the Czech Embassy in London.

Tailpiece

From the many other warplanes which crashed in different parts of the Cairngorms, and are remembered on the two memorials, comes the story of an aircraft which crashed into a south corrie of Braeriach. It had been training for a commando raid on a German Heavy Water production factory in a Norwegian Fjord. In memory of the dead pilot, his seat was placed on the summit of Braeriach and remained there for some years during which at least one young climber from Braemar had the privilege of sitting in that seat!

OBSERVER POST

(information from Peter Lyon Nicol, Braemar ROC, printed in Braemar Buzzard No 31, Dec 2013)

As well as military action during WWII, civil defence had a major role to play. The responsibility of the Royal Observer Corps (ROC), was the detection, identification and tracking of aircraft flying over Britain. Before the widespread use of radar, the only way of identifying aircraft was by sound and observation. When the approximate height of a plane plus the distance and angle from a set point was known, it was possible to calculate its direction, height and approximate position. Observer Posts were set up throughout the land to operate on a 24-hour, 7 day a week basis. Each had two trained ROC members on duty at any time who could pass information to their Command Centre of approaching aircraft and, in particular, warning of enemy aircraft.

The WWII Observer Post in Braemar was a small concrete structure, mainly open with only a tiny rudimentary shelter area. It can still be seen on the shoulder of Morrone just below Downie's Cottage. The Commanding Officer was Peter Lyon Nicol, headmaster of Braemar school. Some years later he wrote: *My first job was to learn the names, height and distance from the post of every mountain within sight, then learn to recognise every plane that flew in the war, allied and enemy.* The observers were given photographs of all the aircraft in flight, after which they had to learn to identify the planes by the distinctive sound of their engines. In Braemar, aural recognition was particularly important as, with the surrounding mountains, an approaching plane could often be heard before it was seen. Observers in each Post were fiercely proud of their skill and had ongoing identification competitions with neighbouring Observer Posts!

The observer's job, however, was most often to track Allied 'strays' who had become lost often on their return from a mission or on training flights. Sadly, even with help from the Observer Post, some of these planes crashed as they were unable to maintain enough height or visibility to avoid the mountains. Happily, there were successes too. Peter described one moonlight night when *we guided a Wellington safely home to Lossiemouth. With a 'wonky' engine, he was lost until we picked him up. He landed safely then asked "How did you know where we were?" When he was told he had been picked up by the ROC he asked the usual question "And who the hell are they?"*

The uniform of the ROC was a steel helmet and a blue and white vertically striped armband, both with the letters 'OC' stencilled on them. In addition, they were given a good pair of navy-issue binoculars. In Braemar the observers had to be strong and dedicated as they were in the Observer Post day and night through summer and winter where temperatures could drop to around -22°C. There were some consolations: every morning before school, two Braemar children collected milk from the dairy in little metal cans and wheeled it in a hurley (cart) up the steep track to the Observer Post; and, as Peter Nicol wrote, *I have happy memories of wading through deep snow and then scrambling up the hill in severe winters. To compensate we had some of the finest scenery in the world around us and in the spring, climbing through the woods, the wonderful scent of the birch trees and sometimes the thrill of coming on a fawn, lying under a tree'.*

A WWII observer calculating an aircraft's position

Braemar WWII Observer Post on Morrone

BRAEMAR HOME GUARD

In 1940 the fear that Hitler would invade Britain was at its height. The coastline of Aberdeenshire was identified as a possible target for German landings and, despite its distance from the sea, Braemar was seen as an important defensive point if invaders moved inland to attack the central belt from the north.

Many troops and masses of equipment and supplies had been left behind in the evacuation from Dunkirk. To support the depleted regular army in defending the country against invading forces, a Home Guard (originally known as Local Defence Volunteers) was mobilised by the Government. Very soon a Home Guard unit was set up and active in most towns and villages across Britain. At its peak, the Home Guard had over 1.7 million part-time soldiers. Braemar's Home Guard was a Section of 8-10 volunteers, part of a 'Battle Platoon' (probably Ballater or Upper Deeside) and were under the command of Sergeant Tommy McPherson and, second in command, Sergeant William (Bill) Brown. The Platoon's Company headquarters were in Banchory, as part of the 3rd (South Aberdeenshire & Kincardineshire) Battalion. The Battalion was affiliated to the Gordon Highlanders.

The Home Guard volunteers, mostly men, were normally either too old (over 40) or too young (under 18) to serve in the armed forces. Many of them had regular jobs during the day and would drill and train at night. They were given uniforms and an armband with 'Home Guard' or LDV (Local Defence Volunteers) printed on it. As most did not possess or could not be supplied with a firearm, the community was often asked to supply rifles, shotguns and pistols. The final resort was to fashion knives and other makeshift 'weapons' from farming implements and other local materials.

At one point, pikes were supplied to the Aberdeenshire battalions. The report by the 4th (City of Aberdeen) Battalion sums up the Home Guard opinion of these weapons: 'By the time the issue of the celebrated pikes was made, the Battalion was well equipped with small arms, so these survivals of Flodden were stowed in the armouries until eventually disposed of as salvage. The Home Guard opinion of the pike was that it was better than nothing and that, used in conjunction with a grenade in close fighting on a dark night, it might well be a means of acquiring a better weapon.' One wonders as to the source of this supply of pikes. Might there be castles or fortified houses in Aberdeenshire still lamenting their loss?

The Home Guard – affectionately known as 'Dad's Army' – was initially assigned to guard essential buildings and transport links against sabotage by fifth columnists (Nazi sympathisers, if any, among the local populace) or attack by parachutists and invaders from the sea. As the home defences were built up, the Home Guard also became responsible for manning a network of roadblocks and look out points. 'Vigilance' was their watchword!

In the event of invasion, the Home Guard would have been expected to support the regular army by defending their village and strong points 'to the last man'. Apart from frustrating movement and progress of enemy forces, the Home Guard would be expected to make sure that civilians did not panic or get in the way of the regular army.

Devil's Elbow WWII remaining 'pillbox'

Sergeant Bill Brown's day job was foreman for Aberdeenshire Council at the Lion's Face Quarry. There he supervised the quarrying and transporting to Aberdeen of very hard quartz 'chips' which were fashioned into concrete slabs 36" square by 4" thick. Once fitted to decks of trawlers, the slabs provided protection against strafing from low flying enemy aircraft.

Bill also worked alongside the Royal Engineers and the Pioneer Corps to construct defensive strongpoints for the village and district. Braemar and the Cairnwell pass were part of a line of defences, known as the Cowie Stop Line, stretching from Stonehaven to Drumochter.

The largest features close to Braemar were two lines of large concrete blocks at the Devil's Elbow

Remaining Anti-Tank Cubes at Devil's Elbow
© Gordon J Barclay (2005). Proceedings of the Society of Antiquaries of Scotland, vol 135

designed to bring to a halt any German tanks and vehicles trying to use the Cairnwell Pass as a route south to the central belt. Many of these anti-tank cubes can still be seen from the old A93 road. On the other, western side of the road, is the still intact 'northern' pillbox (gun emplacement bunker). A second southern pillbox was removed when the A93 was realigned to bypass the Devil's Elbow.

The Braemar Home Guard, like most others, took their duties very seriously. To guard the roads in and out of Braemar, three lookout defence bunkers or trenches were manned by the Home Guard round the clock, 7 days a week. The remains of one trench, to defend Braemar from the east, can still be seen on the lower slopes of Creag Choinnich on the path from the Lion's Face Quarry to Braemar Castle. One can only imagine how cold and boring it must have been waiting in these defences for an invasion and enemies who never arrived.

In early 1941 Hitler gave up plans to invade Britain and turned his armies east to invade Russia. Fixed defences and strong points were no longer required. There was, however, still enough of a threat of small-scale raids and sabotage to keep the Home Guard on the alert and to make their presence felt in the village with training and drills – such as bayonet practice and setting ambushes. On one occasion Sergeant Brown led a full tilt bayonet charge over the golf course and storming across the river. On reaching the far bank he turned round to find everyone else halted suddenly on the other bank of the river without getting their boots wet and staring incredulously at him. It is not reported what the indignant Sergeant Brown did next! Home Guard sections in the area also competed with each other in shooting contests, for which there was a Deeside League with results reported in the Aberdeen Evening Express.

Letters dated January/February 1942 from the insurance company for the Invercauld Arms Hotel to the Invercauld Estate Office raised concern about the 'quantity of Molotov Cocktails' (incendiary grenades) and phosphorus bombs being stored by the Braemar Home Guard in one of the garages of the Invercauld Arms Hotel near to a petrol store. Assurance was soon given by Sergeant McPherson that there were no phosphorus bombs and that the Home Guard would 'construct a small explosives store somewhere about Braemar' for the 'Molotov Cocktails'. Hopefully, the move was achieved quickly because, at this point, the hotel was being used as the school for around 100 Belgian evacuee children!

PART 2 - BRAEMAR WAR MEMORIAL

By the end of World War I nearly every community in Scotland had decided to erect its own War Memorial. Braemar War Memorial was unveiled on 5 October 1921 by HRH Princess Louise, the Princess Royal and by HRH Princess Maud. Between three and four hundred people attended the ceremony to unveil the Celtic cross hewn from local granite. All of Braemar's churches were represented at the ceremony which was also attended by Colonel A H Farquharson of Invercauld and about 40 ex-servicemen. The names of the war dead from World War II were added to the memorial after 1945 with a new plaque listing all of the known Braemar war dead of both World Wars.

Not all the young men commemorated on the War Memorial served in local or even Scottish regiments; some were in the RAF or Mercantile Marine or in Commonwealth regiments. In addition to the men lost, many were injured and traumatised but we have not been able to include their stories here despite their sacrifices. Others quietly returned and resumed their civilian lives.

WORLD WAR I (THE GREAT WAR) 1914-1918

Descent into World War I in 1914 was triggered by events in the Balkans where Austria-Hungary and Ottoman Turkey had been engaged in armed conflict with Serbia and Greece for some years. The spark that ignited war was the assassination of Archduke Franz Ferdinand of Austria on 28 June 1914 by a Serbian terrorist in Sarajevo, Bosnia, which Austria-Hungary had annexed as recently as 1908. Holding Serbia responsible for the assassination, Austria-Hungary, with encouragement from Germany, declared war on Serbia on 28 July 1914. Russia mobilized its army to support Serbia and Germany pre-emptively declared war on Russia and on France as the ally of Russia.

Great Britain and the British Empire entered the war as an ally of France and Russia on 4 August when Germany refused to withdraw its invading troops from Belgium, whose neutrality had been guaranteed by all the Great Powers.

The complicated system of global alliances before the war drew other countries into the conflict. The Allied (Entente) powers – France, Great Britain, and Russia – were joined by

Japan in 1914, Italy in 1915 and Romania in 1916. The Central Powers – Germany and Austria-Hungary – were joined at the outset of the war by the Ottoman Empire of Turkey and in 1915 by Bulgaria. The USA joined the war on the side of the Allied Powers in April 1917 and started to send troops to the Western Front after Germany resumed unrestricted submarine attacks on US and other shipping in the Atlantic.

TO THE GLORY OF GOD
AND IN MEMORY OF THE MEN OF BRAEMAR
WHO GAVE THEIR LIVES IN THE TWO WARS
1914 – 1918   1939 – 1945

WILLIAM ANDERSON	WILLIAM MACDONALD	RUSSELL BELL
CHARLES BONNER	PETER MACHARDY	JOHN EWAN
ROBERT H. BONNER	JAMES MACKINTOSH	JAMES FERGUSON
ROBERT J. CUMMING	DONALD MACKENZIE	CHARLES GRANT
ROSS S. EGGO	CHARLES A. MACLAREN	WILLIAM JOLLY
WILLIAM G. GEDDES	ROBERT PRATT	ALISTAIR LAMONT
JACK GRANT	ANDREW SMITH	ANDREW LAMONT
JAMES INNES	WILLIAM SUMMERS	IAN MACHARDY
ALEX. LAMONT	PATRICK THORNTON	JOHN SCOTT
ALEX. MOLLISON		ROBERT STEWART
ALEX. MACDONALD		CHARLES THOM

THEIR NAME LIVETH FOR EVERMORE

THE OPENING BATTLES OF THE FRONTIERS: AUGUST - SEPTEMBER 1914

All the initial participants mobilised for a quick, decisive victory and expected the war to be 'over by Christmas'. None was prepared for the massive carnage and deadlock to continue for four years in the west and three years in the east.

Germany had long prepared for an aggressive war on two fronts. Immediately war was declared, Germany invaded neutral Belgium in order to attack France in the north. The German advance pushed back the newly arrived British Expeditionary Force (BEF) from Belgium and nearly reached Paris. Then France mounted a massive but failed offensive further south in Lorraine. On the eastern front, Russia attacked German East Prussia and Austria-Hungary in Galicia.

THE WESTERN FRONT: 1914 - 1918

War of Movement: September - October 1914

For a month, in the west, massive armies had manoeuvrered in open field but gradually got bogged down as machine guns, artillery and trenches gave the advantage to defensive deployment. In early September, the German advance in Northern France was halted and reversed by hastily reinforced French troops and British troops who turned the German right flank at the Battle of Marne.

After their initial success, French forces and the BEF tried to outflank the Germans to the north in a series of engagements which have become known as the 'race to the sea'. The Allies sought to advance towards

Belgium in the first Battle of Ypres in October where units of the British Territorial Army took part in the fighting for the first time. Although the initial gains at Ypres were then lost, the Allies succeeded in safeguarding control of the ports of Dunkirk and Calais.

London Scottish routing Vaunted Bavarians in Bayonet Charge
War Illustrated 14 Nov 1914

First Battle of Ypres: 19 October - 22 November 1914

The Gordon Highlanders

Many men from Braemar joined the 'local' regiment, the Gordon Highlanders. They were originally the 100th Regiment of Foot, raised by Alexander, 4th Duke of Gordon in 1794 from local Gordon estates. The regiment has a long tradition of recruitment in North East Scotland and a proud reputation for courage and tenacity in combat. During the Great War, around 50,000 men served with the Gordons in some capacity and the regiment had nine battalions on the Western Front from 1914-18. They gained 65 Battle Honours but at the cost of 29,000 casualties and 9,000 deaths.

2nd Gordons at Gheluvelt

The 2nd Battalion Gordon Highlanders were part of the 7th Division of the British Army, known as the "Immortal Seventh". On 5 October, they sailed from Southampton landing at Zeebrugge in Belgium on 7 October. We know from letters that they were constantly marching and fighting from when they disembarked. They marched through Ostend, Bruges and Ghent with the intention of defending Antwerp. However, Antwerp was already falling under a German attack, so they were ordered to hold key positions near Ypres to support the evacuation of the Belgian Army towards the west. They arrived in Ypres on 14 October where fewer than 30,000 men were holding 240,000 Germans at bay.

On 18 October, the Germans attacked. From 21 October onwards, the 2nd Gordons were under heavy fire and they repulsed several attacks over the next few days. On 28 October, they were ordered to take up unprepared positions near the village of Gheluvelt. They numbered 26 officers and 812 men.

Early the next morning, there was a tremendous German artillery barrage. It was a very foggy morning and before anyone knew what was happening, the 2nd Gordons were overwhelmed by the enemy forces. They withdrew at nightfall in torrential rain. Of the 812 men, 100 were killed, wounded or missing. Losses were terrible again on 30 and 31 October. By 1 November, the 2nd Gordons numbered only 3 officers and 205 men. They retired for rest and refitting on 6 November.

The Gordons were awarded two Victoria Crosses during the Battle of Ypres — Drummer William Kenny from Drogheda, Ireland and Captain James Anson Otho Brooke from Cults, Aberdeen.

London Scottish at Messines Ridge

The London Scottish were volunteers recruited as the 1/14th Battalion London Regiment. They were the first unit of the new Territorial Army to see frontline service on the Western Front.

They arrived at Ypres on 29 October 1914 and spent the next two days digging trenches. But they were then sent up the line to Messines Ridge to plug a gap in the Allied frontline south of Ypres with bayonet charges.

The battle of Ypres ended on 22 November. The BEF had stemmed the attack but lost 8,631 officers and men, 37,264 were wounded and 40,342 were missing. Three men from Braemar were among the dead — **Robert J Cumming, William Summers** and **Andrew Smith.**

The artist Snaffles usually cartooned officers but in 1914 he was inspired to portray the Gordon Highlanders with a stoical old sergeant who with his unruffled attitude sums up the public perception of the regiment as fearless and professional. Jock's face looks as if it was based on that of Drummer Kenny who was the first VC winner of the regiment in Oct 1914.
The Gordon Highlanders Museum, Aberdeen

Gordon Highlanders at start of war
The Gordon Highlanders Museum, Aberdeen

Robert J Cumming *(Service Number 10281)*

Private, 2nd Battalion Gordon Highlanders
Killed in Action on 29 October 1914, aged 27
Commemorated on Ypres (Menin Gate) Memorial, Panel 38

Robert James Cumming, the son of William and Robina Cumming of 5 Castleton Terrace, Braemar was born in Braemar in April 1887. His father was a general labourer and later a stonebreaker. Robert, 18 years old, was living in Glenmuick, Ballater and had been working as a plumber when he enlisted in November 1906 in the 3rd Battalion Gordon Highlanders. Quite why he purchased his discharge for £3 the following month and then re-enlisted in January 1907 is not known. In 1909 he was serving with William Summers (see below) in India with the 2nd Battalion of the Gordon Highlanders.

Robert was still with the 2nd Gordon Highlanders when they were sent to Belgium in 1914. He fought in the first Battle of Ypres and was reported missing near Ypres on 27 October 1914. This listing was later changed to 'died in the field', probably because his body was never found.

Robert J Cumming

William Summers *(Service Number 9927)*

Private, 2nd Battalion Gordon Highlanders
Killed in Action on 28 October 1914, aged 32
Commemorated on Ypres (Menin Gate) Memorial, Panel 38

William was the son of John Summers, labourer, from Felagie, Braemar. William was born in Pannanich, Ballater on September 1882. His mother, Jane, was a domestic servant. It is likely that he enlisted with the Gordon Highlanders around 1907 as he had served in India with the 2nd Gordons as a farrier. At the start of WWI, William went with them to Belgium. He was killed in action on 28 October 1914 near Ypres.

Andrew Smith (Service Number 1823)

Private, 1/14th Battalion London Regiment (London Scottish)
Killed in Action on 1 November 1914, aged 20
Commemorated on Ypres (Menin Gate) Memorial, M.R. 29, Panel 54

Andrew, son of Andrew and Mary Smith, was born in Lamington, Lanarkshire in July 1894 where his father was a farmer. In 1900, the family moved to Altdouray, Braemar when Andrew (senior) became factor on the Invercauld Estate. Young Andrew left school in 1912 and worked for Messrs Steele Brothers, East India merchants, London, intending to go to Rangoon.

He joined the London Scottish on arrival in London and the regiment was

Andrew Smith

called to action when war was declared. He went to France in September 1914 and spent time assisting the Royal Army Medical Corps. He was first reported wounded and a prisoner in Germany but six months later the German authorities admitted their error, having confused him with someone of the same name. The London Scottish had fought in the battle of Messines part of the first Ypres offensive and Andrew appears to have lost his life during that battle.

War of Stalemate and Attrition: November 1914 - February 1918

By November 1914, both sides had dug into lines of trenches extending from the North Sea to Switzerland. The war of movement degenerated into a war of attrition lasting until March 1918 in which small gains were made, and frequently lost again, with very heavy loss of life and equipment.

Saving the guns at Ypres
War Illustrated 6 Feb 1915

The Germans occupied large sections of France (Champagne, Alsace, Lorraine) and Belgium (Flanders), including areas of major coal reserves which were vital for the war economy. Germany was determined to retain these lands and gain access to the Channel Ports while France and Belgium, supported by Britain, were desperate to win back the invaded lands and the Belgian ports of Zeebrugge and Ostend. By 1915 the Germans had established extremely strong defence behind lines of barbed wire, trenches, and fortified machine-gun posts and were intent on holding what they had gained. New weapons such as tanks, massive underground mines, and poison gas were put to use without decisive advantage.

For nearly three years there was continuous fighting punctuated by major offensives but little movement all along the Western Front. Allied generals, supported by politicians still eager for victory, persisted in the belief that massed, frontal assaults by infantry, preceded by massive artillery barrages could achieve a decisive breakthrough into the enemy's rear. In practice, defence artillery and machine guns inflicted massive casualties and defenders were then able to counterattack exhausted and depleted attackers. British and Commonwealth troops were thrown forward in a series of major battles in Belgium and North East France – Ypres II, Artois, Loos, Somme I, Arras, and Ypres III (Passchendaele). In every case, small gains incurring huge loss of life were reversed by German counterattacks.

Some of the British offensives were undertaken on unfavourable terrain in order to draw German reserves away from French armies in other parts of the front. By 1916 the Germans at Verdun and then General Haig in Flanders in 1917 pressed on with stalled offensives whose only purpose was to 'bleed the enemy dry'. Attrition became the justification for continued but hopeless attacks by both sides. Some French soldiers at Verdun refused to continue attacking the Germans but their mutiny was short-lived and undetected by the Germans. By late 1917, the prospect on the Western Front seemed to be continued stalemate with naval blockade the best hope of victory for both sides.

Second Battle of Ypres: 22 April - 25 May 1915

The 2nd Battle of Ypres was fought over control of the Flemish town of Ypres which was held by the Allies and stood in the way of Germany's planned sweep from the north across the last part of Belgium and into France.

During this battle, in April 1915, the German Army first used chlorine gas. Newly arrived Canadian infantrymen were particularly badly affected and among their dead, later in the battle, was **Alex McDonald**, formerly of Braemar. The soldiers had no protection, as gas masks were not issued until July 1915. Instead, the Canadians were advised to make masks from fabric, such as towels, hankies, socks or belts on which they should urinate, as ammonia was erroneously thought to neutralise the chlorine!

A report in The Daily Chronicle of 26 April 1915 sums up the horror of the gas attack:

The . . . soldiers were naturally taken by surprise. Some got away in time, but many, alas not understanding the new danger, were not so fortunate, and were overcome by the fumes and died poisoned. Among those who escaped nearly all cough and spit blood, the chlorine attacking the mucous membrane. The dead were turned black at once. About 15 minutes after letting the gas escape the Germans got out of their trenches. Some of them were sent on in advance, with masks over their heads, to ascertain if the air had become breathable. Having discovered that they could advance, they arrived in large numbers in the area on which the gas had spread itself some minutes before, and took possession of the arms of the dead men. They made no prisoners. Whenever they saw a soldier whom the fumes had not quite killed they snatched away his rifle and advised him to lie down "to die better".

On 3 May 1915, the 1/7th Gordon Highlanders landed at Boulogne where they joined the 153rd Brigade in the 51st Highland Division. On 19 May, they moved to the front line and gained their first experience of digging into the Flanders mud to consolidate their position. The soldiers found, however, that they could not dig down sufficiently because of the water and so had to build up breastworks to provide protection.

The 2nd Battle of Ypres was finally ended by the Germans who wanted to transfer troops to reinforce the defence against the major Allied offensive to the south in Artois. The Germans had gained little from the Battle of Ypres. They did not achieve their objective of capturing the town, which was virtually destroyed by the bombing, but did manage to push back the Allied front line three miles closer to Ypres.

Ypres wounded attended by Royal Army Medical Corps - by Gilbert Rogers

Alexander McDonald (Alex) *(Service Number 27145)*

Sergeant, 15th Battalion (48th Highlanders), 3rd Brigade, 1st Canadian Division,
Canadian Expeditionary Force
Killed in Action on 27 April 1915, aged 28
Commemorated on St Julien Memorial and Ypres (Menin Gate) Memorial, Panel 18-24-26-30

Alex McDonald was born at home in 2 Fern Cottage, Braemar in November 1886 (and not 1888 as later claimed on his enlistment documentation). He subsequently grew up there with his two sisters, Mary and

Jessie. His parents were Alexander McDonald, a jobbing gardener and later mole catcher, and Marjory McDonald (ms McHardy). It is likely that, before the 1911 census, Alex had emigrated to Canada where he worked as a lineman installing and repairing telegraph lines.

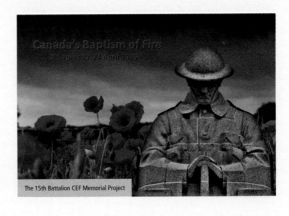

The 15th Battalion CEF Memorial Project

On 18 September 1914, Alex enlisted as a private in the 15th Battalion (48th Highlanders of Canada). With both his parents dead, his younger sister Jessie, who was still living in Fern Cottage, Braemar, was named as his next of kin.

Within a month, Alex was on his way to France as part of the Canadian Expeditionary Force (CEF) arriving in France on 15 February 1915. Before then, Alex had received promotion to Sergeant. At Ypres, he served in No2 Company as an infantry rifleman probably in charge of either a Platoon or Section. It is very likely that he experienced the first gas attack before being killed in action a few days later on 27 April 1915. Alex's name is engraved on the St Julien Memorial which commemorates the participation of the Canadian First Division in the Second Battle of Ypres.

The Artois Offensive: 16 May - 30 June 1915

By May 1915, the Germans had created a salient (bulge) in the front line which was threatening the communications between Paris and sections of Northern France. The Artois Offensive was a joint British and French operation to remove this threat and also to cut the rail link which transported supplies to the German front line. Part of the British sector of the offensive was a battle fought at the town of Festubert during which **Alex Lamont** from Braemar died of wounds.

Cameronians attempting to disperse gas with Vermorel sprayer, Artois 1915

In the Artois Offensive, the allies gained only a small amount of ground and none of the high ground they had aimed to capture nor did they succeed in cutting the German rail link. The cost in loss of men and equipment on both sides far outweighed any gain.

Alexander Lamont (Service Number 2317)

Corporal, 1/7th Gordon Highlanders
Died of Wounds on 23 September 1915, aged 23
Buried at Millencourt Communal Cemetery Extension

Alexander, born in Braemar in 1891, was the son of Mary and Andrew Lamont (a crofter) of Rosebank, Braemar and had three brothers and two sisters. He was a house painter living at home in Braemar when, around 1909, he joined the Gordon Highlanders Territorial Force.

In August 1914, Alexander enlisted at Banchory and served as Corporal Lamont, an Infantryman with the 1/7th Gordon Highlanders. In May 1915 he spent 10 days in a casualty hospital with an ankle problem exacerbated by rheumatism before returning to his unit. On 20 June 1915 he was wounded near Festubert and transferred to the Casualty Clearing Station on 6 July. He died of wounds on 23 September 1915, probably in the Millencourt Field Hospital.

Machine Gun Corps team wearing anti-gas helmets
CC-BY-SA

Battle of Loos:
25 September - 8 October 1915

The Battle of Loos, the largest British attack of 1915, was aimed at breaking the stasis of the trench warfare. It was the first time Britain used volunteers, many of whom were Scottish and many with little training, in a major battle. It was also the first battle in which Britain used poison gas (chlorine gas). Douglas Haig, the commanding General, felt that gas, which Britain had previously condemned, might give his raw recruits some additional 'cover' from the German machine gunners.

Sadly, the British supportive artillery bombardment proved insufficient and the British gas failed to wreak the expected damage on the German defence. Unfavourable winds caused the gas to linger in 'no-man's land' through which the attackers had to pass and some of it even blew back into the British trenches. Thus, despite being better supplied with ammunition and equipment, the British suffered defeat. German machine-guns and extensive use of barbed wire further contributed to the disaster. There were 50,000 British casualties between the 25 and 28 September. Of the 21,000 killed, 7,000 were Scots including **William Geddes** from Braemar.

William George Geddes *(Service Number 18329)*

Private, 13th Battalion Royal Scots
Died on 26 September 1915, aged 26
Commemorated on the Loos Memorial M.R., Panel 10-13 and Braemar Cemetery

William George Geddes was born at Alt-na-Clunie in Braemar in May 1889. He was the son of Peter Stevenson, a general merchant in Braemar, and Lavinia Geddes (ms Smith). William, who enlisted in North Berwick, was an infantryman with the 13th Battalion Royal Scots and was killed on 26 September 1915. His wife, at the time, was living in Stirling.

Battle of the Somme: 1 July - 18 November 1916 (and post battle phase to end March 1917)

The Battle of the Somme was a landmark battle. It was a joint French/British offensive planned to combine with simultaneous offensives on the Russian and Italian fronts and aimed to hasten the end of the war.

The British High Command was overconfident of the ability of its massive artillery barrage to suppress defences and unaware of how much the Germans had learned of their plans and how well they had prepared for the expected attack. The cost to the Allied infantry on the first day was horrendous with the worst losses of men on one day in the history of the British army – 57,470 casualties of whom 19,240 were killed. In the days that followed, the Germans fought on and the casualty and death toll continued to rise. Included among the Somme dead were three men from Braemar **James Innes, William McDonald** and **Donald MacKenzie**. In addition, **Charles Bonner**, formerly of Braemar, died in the post Somme phase.

When the battle ended on 18 November, the Allies had moved six miles into German territory but had failed to gain most of their key objectives. The new German commander had merely withdrawn his army to a position (the Hindenburg Line) which, being shorter in length than the previous German front line, could provide stronger defences. At the time, the Battle of the Somme was considered to be a hard-won victory against a brave, experienced opponent. Over the years, however, given the horrendous number of casualties and loss of life, the view has changed to one of its being a bloody and futile battle.

Several salutary lessons, however, were learned. In planning the Somme Offensive, the Allies had seriously underestimated the German defences including the strength of the barbed wire and the depth of their trenches which enabled them to withstand considerable pounding. This was also the first major battle for many of the inexperienced 'Pals' battalions specially recruited for Lord Kitchener's 'new army' where friends and colleagues were encouraged to enlist and serve together. But when heavy casualties occurred in a Pals unit a generation of young men from one village or area were decimated.

Other lessons were more positive. This was the first battle where tanks were used. Although rather unreliable because of their newness, and unpleasantly hot for those inside, tanks were clearly a weapon for the future. In addition, aerial reconnaissance by the fledgling Royal Flying Corps was, for the first time, used extensively and successfully in the Battle of the Somme.

British trench, Battle of the Somme 1916

15 September 1916, day Allied tanks first used

James Innes *(Service Number 3820)*

Private, 1/9th Battalion, The King's Liverpool Regiment
Killed in Action on 16 July 1916, aged 22
Commemorated on the Arras Memorial M. R. 20 Bay 3.

James Thomson Innes, born in Braemar in September 1894, was the son of John Innes and Jane Innes (ms Thomson) of Millington Cottage, Braemar. John was a carrier who, at the time of James' death was foreman with Captain Milne, railway carrier and contractor in Braemar. James was a baker. He served his apprenticeship in Aboyne and, before joining the army, was a baker with a firm in Liverpool.

James had only been in France for a fairly short time when he was killed in fierce fighting in the Battle of the Somme on 16 July 1916. He has no known grave.

William MacDonald *(Service Number 4746)*

Private, 8th Battalion Black Watch
Died of Wounds on 20 August 1916, aged 34
Buried in Abbeville Communal Cemetery, Somme, Memorial reference III.B.20.

William, the eldest son of Ellen and Ewen McDonald (later of Tordarroch, West Cults, Aberdeenshire), and was born in 1881 at The Knock, Inverey, Braemar where his father was gamekeeper. He was recorded as a carpenter's apprentice in the 1901 census and then seems to have gone to England in 1905 to join the police, where he did not settle and resigned in 1906.

As a private in the 8th Battalion Black Watch (named "Jocks and Springboks" after they were joined by the 1st South Africa Battalion early in 1916), William was part of Kitchener's 'New Army'. In addition, William was a member of the Regimental Police (RP), as can be seen in his photo from the RP insignia on the left cuff of his uniform. In this role, William would have had responsibility for the maintenance of good order and military discipline and for passing on criminal offences to the Royal Military Police.

William arrived in France on 10 May 1915 and, two days later on 12 May, left Boulogne by train for the Western Front. He is likely to have taken part in all the operations involving the battalion, including the Battle of Loos on 27 September 1915. It was during the Battle of Delville Wood (July-Sept 1916, part of the Battle of the Somme) that William was wounded in action as his name appeared on the Casualty List of 21 August 1916. If he had lived, this would have meant he was authorised to wear a "Wound Stripe", a 2-inch vertical strip on the left jacket sleeve. Sadly, on 20 August, the day before the publication of the Casualty List, William had died as a result of these wounds. He was aged 34.

William MacDonald

Donald MacKenzie *(Service Number 8/2078)*

Private, 8th Southland Company, 1st Battalion Otago Regiment, New Zealand
Expeditionary Force (NZEF)
Died on 27 September 1916, aged 27
Buried in Caterpillar Valley Cemetery, Longueval, Somme.

Donald was born in Braemar in January 1888. He was the son of James Brown MacKenzie, a shepherd and later a road surfaceman of Braemar, and Sarah Jane MacKenzie (ms Horn). As no trace so far has been found of Donald in the 1911 census, it is quite possible that he had emigrated to New Zealand before then. In WWI, he served with the 8th Southland Company, Otago Regiment, NZEF. He was wounded in the Gallipoli campaign in 1915 but was serving again with his regiment at the Battle of the Somme where he was killed in September 1916.

Charles Bonner *(Service Number 42149)*

Private, 2nd Battalion, King's Own Yorkshire Light Infantry
Killed in Action on 7 March 1917, aged 27
Commemorated at the Rosières Communal Cemetery Extension Fr 0649 Plot III Row C Grave 7

Charles, born in Castleton, Braemar in November 1883, was the son of Alexander, originally a mail contractor who later became a farmer, and Elizabeth Bonner (ms Henderson) of Creag Choinnich, Braemar. In 1901 Charles was recorded as a farmer's son and, at the time of his marriage to Margaret Fraser Forsyth in August 1904, as a farm servant. By 1911, however, he with his wife and three daughters were living in Gateshead where he was a railway porter.

Charles enlisted at Gateshead in what was formerly the 32/846, Northumberland Fusiliers. During much of WWI, he served with the King's Own Yorkshire Light Infantry. On 7 March 1917, Charles was killed at Ancre in Picardy pursuing the Germans, who were retreating to their new defensive position on the Hindenburg Line after the Battle of the Somme.

Bath found in German dugout!
War Illustrated 4 Nov 1916

Battle of Arras: 9 April - 4 May 1917

The Battle of Arras was a battle the British Commander-in-Chief did not wish to fight. Earl Haig wanted the British and Commonwealth emphasis to remain in the north protecting Ypres, clearing the Belgian coastline (used by German submarines) and capturing the German railhead so vital for their war supplies. Instead he was over-ruled by the agreement of the new UK Prime Minister, Lloyd George, to provide support to the French who were planning a massive attack which they were convinced would bring the 'breakthrough' and hasten the end of the war. An attack by the British on Arras would divert some German resources from the main French operation a little to the south.

Using experience gained from the Somme, the British and Commonwealth troops were given considerable pre-training and preparation assisted by maps and information from RFC air reconnaissance missions.

Royal Flying Corps reconnaissance 1917
National Army Museum

In addition, engineers dug deep tunnels from the rear to the front of the line enabling the men to move forward safely.

The initial attack, preceded by an artillery barrage for a full week plus a gas attack, progressed well. The British were able to advance about three and a half miles and the Canadians, despite vigorous German opposition resulting in significant casualties and deaths, captured the Vimy Ridge (a major target of the operation). The battle then degenerated into the usual stalemate with very few additional gains being made.

Despite neither the British nor the French achieving the desired breakthrough, the Battle of Arras was considered a victory for the Allies because of the small gains they did achieve. The cost in human lives was, however, very great, particularly after the first couple of days. The death toll was massive and there were huge numbers wounded or gassed. Included in the deaths were two men with Braemar connections **Ross Eggo** and **Alexander Mollison** plus **Patrick Thornton** who died a year later of complications from wounds received during the Battle of Arras.

Ross Eggo

Ross Stewart Eggo *(Service Number 265097)*

Private, 1/6th Perthshire Battalion Black Watch (Royal Highlanders)
Killed in action on 23 April 1917, aged 22
Buried at Brown's Copse Cemetery, Roeux FR0604 Plot 1 Row D Grave 34 and remembered in Braemar Kirk.

Ross Stewart Eggo, born in July 1894 in Braemar, was the eldest of 5 children of John and Euphemia Benton Eggo of Craig Cottage, Braemar. Mr Eggo was a tailor and draper. Before enlisting in Blairgowrie, Ross worked as a grocer's messenger in Braemar. He was involved in the Arras offensive and was killed during the capture and subsequent loss of the Roeux chemical works.

Alexander Mollison *(Service Number 20800)*

Private, 10th Battalion, Canadian Infantry, Alberta Regiment
Killed in Action on 1 May 1917, aged 32
Buried at the Ecoivres Military Cemetery, Mont-Saint-Eloi: V.H.17

Alexander, born in February 1885 in Braemar, was the son of Harry (Henry) Mollison a master mason and his wife Annie Mollison (ms McDonald). Harry sadly died in 1893 when Alexander was only 8 years. In 1901 Annie is recorded as a laundress and Alexander was working as an apprentice carpenter. At some point in the early years of the century, Alexander emigrated to Canada, probably to Alberta, where he worked as a local fireman.

Alexander enlisted in the Alberta Regiment of the Canadian Infantry and served with them in France. He was listed as wounded on 23 April 1915 when he was treated for a gunshot wound to the left foot but discharged fairly soon thereafter as he was back with his regiment on 1 May 1917 when he was killed during the attack on Vimy Ridge in the Battle of Arras.

Patrick Thornton *(Service Number 242532)*

Private, 1/5th Battalion Gordon Highlanders
Died on 10 August 1918, aged 29
Buried in St Andrew's Graveyard, Braemar, South East Part, 123.3

Patrick was born in Glasgow in 1889, the son of Mary Thornton. Before the war, he was a farm labourer lodging in Little Inverey with Angus Grant, a crofter and estate labourer. Patrick joined the 1/5th Gordon Highlanders on 8 February 1916, conscription having begun in January 1916.

It was during the final days of the Battle of Arras on 16/17 May 1916, in a counterattack on the Roeux chemical works that Patrick was seriously wounded. We do not know the nature of his wounds which may have been from the bombardment or from the heavy gas

British and German wounded going together to dressing station, Arras 1917 CC-BY-SA

attack on 16 May experienced by the 6th Gordons, whom Patrick's unit were relieving, or from a combination of both. Whatever the injury, it is unlikely that Patrick was able to return to active service as he was eventually discharged from the Army on 24 December 1917 on account of 'disablement or ill-health caused otherwise than by misconduct', having been proclaimed 'permanently and totally disabled'. Seven months later, on 10 August, Patrick died at Harley Cottage, Inverey of tubercular peritonitis and meningitis, which are very likely to have been infections secondary to his wounds.

When he was honourably discharged, Patrick was given a Silver War Badge (also known as a Discharge Badge, Wound Badge or Services Rendered Badge). The purpose of the badge was to protect former soldiers from being presented with a white feather by some women who gave them out as an implication of cowardice to apparently able-bodied young men not wearing the King's uniform.

Silver War Badge

Third Battle of Ypres – Passchendaele: 31 July - 10 November 1917

The town of Ypres was a battleground through most of WWI because of its proximity to the Channel ports and supply routes for both the Allies and Germany. It and the surrounding low-lying area were in the hands of the Allies but the ridges to the south and east of the town were in German hands giving them an excellent position for attack and for observing all movements in the area.

Douglas Haig was convinced that an offensive in summer 1917 would rout the Germans from the ridges, capture the German railhead, vital for their supplies, secure the Channel ports for the Allies and threaten the German submarine bases at Ostend and Zeebrugge. He saw it as a 'war-winning' campaign. No-one else, however, shared his view. The plan was opposed by Lloyd George and the Chiefs of Staff of Britain and France on the grounds that the predicted gains were overly optimistic and very unlikely to be achieved. They also believed that it was too soon after a major failed French offensive and that Allied resources should await the arrival of the USA troops and that resources should not be moved back up to Flanders. Eventually, however, Douglas Haig gained permission not least because of the pressure from the navy for something to be done to limit the losses of merchant ships from German U-boats.

The initial stage of the battle, the capture of the Messines Ridge, was successful. Sadly, the Allies delayed the follow up attack on the other ridges, thus allowing the Germans time to strengthen their defences. From then, the operation was a disaster with neither side making significant gains. Unseasonal very heavy rain, aggravated by the destruction of the drainage system from repeated bombardments over the years, turned the entire low-lying battlefield into a mud bath. Both sides were bogged down in mud. Equipment was grounded, men drowned and animals died from exhaustion trying to move equipment. In addition, the Germans introduced the use of mustard gas which caused chemical burns.

Attempts to call off the battle at an earlier stage failed as Haig was determined to capture Passchendaele (the name by which this battle is now often known). When the Canadians eventually captured the Passchendaele ridge in November 1917 and the offensive was finally stopped, the Allies had gained very little. They had not achieved the breakthrough, they had not captured the German rail head nor were they in any better position to blockade the German U-boats. Although exact casualty figures are disputed, the loss was huge, including **Robert Pratt** from Braemar. Passchendaele became synonymous with futility, mud and sacrifice of lives.

Attempting to haul 18-pounder field gun from Passchendaele mud

Robert Pratt (Service Number 17208)

Private, 15th Battalion Royal Scots
Killed in action on 21 October 1917, aged 36
Commemorated on the Tyne Cot Memorial M. R. Panel 011 to 014 and 162.

Robert was born at St Mary's, Forfar, son of Joseph Pratt, a tailor, and Agnes Pratt (ms Honeyman). He grew up in Cupar, Fife. By 1901, Robert was a slater living in Ormiston. In June of that year, in Edinburgh, he married Jane Donaldson who was living there as a domestic servant. They had a daughter and a son. By 1911 Robert was a slater in Haddington but by the outbreak of war he was working as a slater on the Invercauld Estate and living in an estate property at the Keiloch.

Robert was killed in action near Ypres during Passchendaele, the Third Battle of Ypres.

Breakout and Victory: March - November 1918

Both sides on the Western front were thoroughly exhausted by the end of 1917. But reinforcements of men and munitions were on the way. The Allies' reinforcements were from the USA, which would eventually commit an army of over two million to the Western front. Germany benefitted from the collapse of Russia with an Armistice ending the war on the Eastern Front in December 1917. The military advantage of numbers swung first in Germany's favour and was then, decisively, reversed by American reinforcement of the Allies.

By early 1918, it was apparent that Germany planned a major Spring Offensive on the Western Front seeking 'victory before the Americans arrive', using large reserves of troops and munitions released from the Eastern Front. Ludendorff's first objective was to roll back and defeat the British Army and seize the French channel ports. New tactics of open warfare – what later became known as Blitzkrieg – were adopted. This was a short and intense 'hurricane' barrage by artillery, followed by a 'creeping' barrage behind which groups of highly trained stormtroopers attacked weak points and swarmed past strong points in the defences. The first attacks were stunningly sudden and assisted by heavy fog.

By early April, the Allied situation for Britain and France was critical; defeat in France seemed a real possibility. The first German attack had advanced nearly 40 miles towards Amiens. Their heavy gun – Big Bertha – was shelling Paris. Haig issued his famous order (11 April) that his army must carry on fighting "with our backs to the wall and believing in the justice of our cause" to protect "the safety of our homes and the freedom of mankind".

The initial gains of ground up to June exceeded Ludendorff's plans but it proved easier to attack than to supply or reinforce the advance. Allied Forces stretched the attacking Germans to their limits of supply and morale by keeping their main strength further back from the front. By attacking across former battlefields in Picardy and Flanders and exposing their flanks, the Germans laid themselves open to counterattack.

British soldiers at mass in the ruined Cambrai Cathedral, Oct 1918

A newly unified command was agreed for the whole Western front under Marshal Foch which launched heavy counterattacks first by the French in July and then the British in August and the Americans in September. From July onwards the story of the Western front is of continuous advance and victories for Allied forces. Ludendorff declared 8 August – the first day of a major British attack east of Amiens – as 'the black day of the German Army'. Even the redoubtable Hindenburg Line of defences was breached by assault.

A break in the demolition clearing in Cambrai, Oct 1918

The war of movement over eight months in 1918 was fiercely intense with very heavy casualties, though there were no 'Braemar' deaths, and large numbers of prisoners were captured on both sides. Germany lost all it had gained in the early months of the war, and more, and was on the brink of collapse and revolution by the time an Armistice was agreed and the guns on the Western Front fell silent on 11 November.

BATTLE OF GALLIPOLI: 17 FEBRUARY 1915 - 9 JANUARY 1916

The Dardanelles campaign of 1915 is one of the most puzzling for us today. Why were so many British, Commonwealth, and French troops committed to capturing the Gallipoli peninsula from Ottoman Turkey at such heavy loss and eventual defeat? The declared motives were to support the ally, Russia, whose Black Sea ports Turkey had precipitately attacked in October 1914 at the instigation of Germany, and to safeguard the sea routes in the eastern Mediterranean and the Suez Canal in Egypt.

In reality, both Britain and France had two other war objectives. One was to attack the south east flank of Germany and its allies (a misconception particularly beloved of Winston Churchill and Lloyd George). But Britain and France also had their eye on territorial gains taking control from Turkey in the Middle East and in what was then called Mesopotamia (it was here that the fabled Lawrence of Arabia instigated Arab uprisings against the Ottoman Turks).

Cutting up captured enemy ammunition to put into empty jam tins to make bombs - Gallipoli

British Soldier fires machine gun with periscope attachment, Gallipoli

The Dardanelles campaign was mishandled from the start first by the Navy and then by the Generals. Admittedly, it was the first large-scale invasion from the sea to face heavy resistance in the landing areas. The idea was to capture the Gallipoli peninsula in order to command the Dardanelles Straits and threaten the Turkish capital, Constantinople. But the terrain was greatly unfavourable to attackers having to advance inland up steep hillsides and ravines in the heat of summer against Turkish troops well trained and equipped by the Germans.

The early landings in April 1915 were made by British and French troops at Cape Helles (the westernmost headland of Gallipoli) and by Australian and New Zealand troops at what became known as Anzac Bay further north east. Although several beachheads were quickly established, onward progress was painfully slow with heavy casualties on both sides. When the 52nd Highland Division arrived in July its volunteer and inexperienced men were pitched into a series of attacks from Cape Helles (known as the three Battles of Krithia) all of which failed.

The third of these engagements was undertaken by two brigades of 52nd Highland division including 5th Battalion Highland Light Infantry attacking in turn what became known as 'Bloody Valley'. The attacks on 12 July, in which **Peter McHardy** from Braemar died, began well with the capture of the first Ottoman trench but 'descended into chaos and confusion as, in a repeat of earlier Helles battles, the troops advanced too far, lost contact and came under artillery and machine gun fire'. 'The next morning confusion and panic resulted in a disorderly retreat' which was eventually halted by troops of the Naval Division.

The Commanding Officer of 52nd Highland division, Major-General Egerton, was outspoken in his criticism of his superiors for ordering these attacks, saying in his later account that they were "premature and unnecessary ... costly and wasteful" and "positively wicked". He was temporarily relieved of his post, but this was the last attempt to advance from Cape Helles.

In August, after further unavailing and infamously costly attempts were made to advance, the whole campaign petered out and was abandoned. The one tactical success was the skilful evacuation of troops from the other beachheads in December and from Cape Helles in January 1916.

Peter McHardy (MacHardy) *(Service Number 2153)*

Private, 6th Battalion, Highland Light Infantry
Died on 12 July 1915, aged 28
Commemorated on the Helles Memorial, M. R. 04 Gallipoli Panel 174-178 and on a gravestone in Braemar Cemetery.

Peter, born in June 1886, was the eldest son of Charles and Jessie McHardy (ms McDonald) of Viewmount Cottage, Braemar and older brother of Walter Lovie McHardy. Charles was described as a feu owner in 1886 and, later, as a retired gamekeeper. In 1911, Peter was living as a boarder in Yoker, Renfrewshire (now Glasgow) where he was a shop assistant.

Peter enlisted in the 6th Battalion, Highland Light Infantry, a unit of the Territorial Force drawing most of its recruits from the Glasgow area, and sailed with them to Gallipoli on 26 May 1915. Like so many others, there was considerable confusion over Peter's ending. His name initially appeared on the Casualty list of the first day's fighting, 12 July 1915, as 'wounded'. The family were notified and a report appeared in the 13 August 1915 Aberdeen Weekly Journal.

On 8 October 1915, the official record was changed to 'wounded and missing'. This record was later further changed to 'Killed in Action on 12 July 1915' and that is the date now recorded in the Official Records. A further complication arises with the date on the family gravestone in Braemar cemetery which states 'Missing in Action 1916'. Since the gravestone was carved very many years after the event, and the regiment was evacuated to Egypt in January 1916, it is likely that someone in Braemar misread a '5' for a '6'.

ITALIAN CAMPAIGN: 24 MAY 1915 - 4 NOVEMBER 1918

At the outset of war in 1914, Italy was allied to Germany and Austria-Hungary in the defensive Triple Alliance but refused to join in the fighting. The promise of territorial gains lured Italy into joining the war on the side of the Allies in 1915 and attacking Austro-Hungarian forces in the mountainous area. For two years there was continuous fighting but stalemate until the Battle of Caporetto in October 1917 when the Austro-

Italians attacking Austro-Hungarian forces in Italian mountains

Manoeuvring into position the type of 6 inch 26 cwt Howitzer Jack would have used

Hungarians routed the main Italian army with the help of reinforcements released from the eastern front and new tactics provided by Germany.

In response, in 1917 the Allies (France, Britain and USA) sent troops and artillery to support Italy. The 23rd Division, which included 35th Brigade Royal Field Artillery, was sent to Italy. In 1918, they were operating as part of XIV Corps of the 10th British-Italian Army on the east flank of the front north of Treviso.

On 24 October 1918, the Allies attacked north to cross the Piave River and drive the Austro-Hungarians back to the Alps. The early days of the battle, known as the Battle of Vittorio Veneto, involved massive artillery duels, during one of which **Jack Grant** from Braemar was killed. The campaign was successful, however, and the Austro-Hungarians were forced into headlong retreat. They ceased hostilities on 3 November and an Armistice with Italy was signed on 4 November.

John Grant (Jack) *(Service number 242702)*

Gunner, 31st Battery, 35th Brigade Royal Field Artillery
Killed in Action on 26 October 1918, aged 22
Buried at Giavera British Cemetery, Plot 2, Row H, Grave 10

Jack Grant, born in Braemar in September 1896, was the son of Donald Grant, a postboy and later a general labourer, and Jane Grant (ms Lamont). In 1911 he was aged 14 and a schoolboy living with his parents and six siblings in Bellevue Cottage, Braemar. He was killed in action in Giavera, north of Treviso in Italy probably on the second day of the Battle of Vittorio Veneto.

SOUTH AFRICAN CAMPAIGN: AUGUST 1914 - JULY 1915

Before the war, European countries competed to gain new colonies in Africa. Britain had secured control of South Africa after the Boer war ending in 1902 but in the 'scramble for Africa' Germany had established colonies just to the north in South West Africa (now Namibia) and East Africa (now Tanzania). These threatened control of the Cape and its vital sea routes to Asia and Australasia.

The elected government of the Union of South Africa dominion committed its army to the British side in the war. But in October 1914 there was a mutiny by Afrikaners still intent on independence from Britain and wishing to side with Germany. This was quickly crushed and released troops to occupy the German colonies to the north. South West Africa fell quickly and Tanganyika (Tanzania) was occupied but the German commander of locally recruited natives, General Lettow-Vorbeck, managed to continue hit and run operations in Mozambique and Northern Rhodesia (Zambia) until the end of the war.

South Africa provided troops for the British armies on the Western front and in the Middle East, but also kept itself on a war footing against the Germans to the north or possible insurrections by the Boers or natives. One of those who died towards the very end of the war was **Robert Bonner** who was born and brought up in Braemar.

Robert Henderson Bonner *(Service number MT/8510)*

Driver, South Africa Service Corps (Mechanical Transport)
Died on 27 October 1918, aged 40
Buried in Thaba Tshwane Military Cemetery (Old No. 1), Gauteng, South Africa 344 c23.

Robert, son of Alexander Bonner, a mail contractor and later a farmer, and Elizabeth Bonner (ms Henderson), was born at Castleton, Braemar on 26 December 1877. He was one of a large family which included his younger brother, Charles Bonner, who died in Flanders in 1917 (see earlier). In 1891, aged 14, Robert was a bank clerk living with his uncle in Fordoun, Kincardine. As there is no trace of Robert in later UK census, and he is described as 'South African' in the war dead records, it seems quite likely that he had emigrated to South Africa at some point after 1891. In 1918, Robert was a driver with the Mechanical Transport Unit of the South Africa Service Corps. Although the unit was also responsible for railways and barges, Robert probably drove a motor vehicle similar to the one shown in the picture. He died of pneumonia on 27 October 1918, most likely while in a 'supporting role' in South Africa rather than on 'active service'. It is possible, but not confirmed, that his pneumonia was a result of Spanish Flu which had reached epidemic proportions in South Africa at that time.

WWI Army Service Corps Motorised Transport
CC-BY-SA

WAR AT SEA: 1914 - 1918

Before the war, naval planners and strategists thought that conflict at sea would be decided by set piece battles between the British and German fleets of battleships. In fact, the main battle fleets had only a brief but large-scale encounter in the Battle of Jutland of 1916 after which the German High Seas Fleet stayed in port. In the early part of the war, a few German surface warships had some success in attacking British merchant shipping in the Atlantic and even the Pacific and Indian oceans but were eventually hunted down and destroyed.

Far more important was the war of blockades by which Britain and Germany tried to deprive each other of imports of munitions and food. The Royal Navy sought to seal off both the Channel and the northern

Sinking of the Linda Blanche merchant ship – January 1915
by Willy Stöwer

entrance to the North Sea by surface vessels and mines. The Germans relied mainly upon submarines to attack British surface warships and merchant ships in the North Sea, Atlantic, and elsewhere.

The blockades were a key element in diplomatic manoeuvres with neutral countries. The most important was the USA (which was brought into the war as a full combatant in 1917 by the precipitate German decision of 'unrestricted' attacks on any vessels trying to reach Britain) but the Scandinavian countries and the Netherlands stayed neutral throughout the war. The 'submarine menace' peaked in mid-1917 but was gradually reduced by the introduction of escorted convoys across the Atlantic, and by much improved anti-submarine technology and tactics.

The increasing numbers and range of German submarines in the Atlantic, and extensive minefields in the Channel and North Sea, presented a serious hazard to merchant shipping and fishing boats. By the end of the War, more than 3,000 British flagged vessels had been sunk and nearly 15,000 merchant seamen had died. Included among them, surprisingly, were three merchant seamen from landlocked Braemar, **William Anderson, Charles McLaren** and also **James McIntosh** who died in 1919 after the end of hostilities when his ship struck a WWI mine which had not been disarmed.

The sea lanes for moving troops and supplies, however, remained open if hazardous for Allied shipping. Restriction of sea borne supplies led to shortages of munitions at the front and rationing of food at home which might have brought the European war to an end in 1917. But the collapse of Russia and entry of USA into the war brought more troops onto the Western front and eased some of the shortages of food in Britain.

Scuttling German Fleet, Scapa flow
1919 - by Theo Matejko

William Anderson

Third Engineer, SS 'Beeswing'
Lost at Sea on 4 March 1915, aged 29
Commemorated on Tower Hill Memorial

William was born in Braemar, son of John and Jane Anderson (ms Morrison) and husband of Isabella Anderson (ms Wallace) of West North Street, Aberdeen. He was a Third Engineer on the SS Beeswing which set sail from Newcastle upon Tyne on 2 March 1915, bound for Dieppe and carrying a large cargo of coal. The SS Beeswing and all hands were never seen again. It is assumed that the ship, like so many others, was sunk by a mine or torpedo. William's date of death is given in the war records as 4 March 1915 and his name is recorded on the Tower Hill Memorial which lists the men of the Merchant Navy and Fishing Fleets who have no grave but the sea.

Charles A McLaren

Wireless Operator, SS 'Santa Amalia', Mercantile Marine
Died at Sea on 28 December 1917, aged 17
Commemorated on the Tower Hill Memorial

Charles, born in Braegarie, Braemar in March 1901, was the eldest of four children and only son of John Grant McLaren, domestic gardener, and Elizabeth McLaren (ms Rush). Charles was a wireless operator with the Mercantile Marine on the SS 'Santa Amalia', part of the Eagle Oil Transport Company. The Santa Amalia had been a dry cargo steamship, originally named the SS Drumlanrig. It was torpedoed and sunk by a U-boat in the Atlantic, west of Islay. Charles was one of 43 officers and crew who perished.

James Donald McIntosh

Wireless Operator, SS 'Northumbria', Mercantile Marine
Died at Sea on 9 January 1919, aged 19
Commemorated on the Tower Hill Memorial

James Donald McIntosh, born in December 1899 in the Ballochbuie, Crathie, was the son of Charles, a gamekeeper on the Balmoral Estate, and Jessie McIntosh (ms Riach). In 1911 Charles and Jessie were living in the Danzig Shiel, Balmoral while 11-year-old James, a scholar, was boarding at Sunnybrae Cottage, Braemar. After the war, James' parents moved to Ellangowan on Chapel Brae, Braemar.

In January 1919, James was serving on the SS 'Northumbria' when it struck two unexploded WWI mines off the English coast near Middlesbrough. The ship was carrying wheat from Baltimore. All the crew managed to escape in lifeboats before the ship sank. Their distress signals were spotted and a rescue attempt begun. Sadly, however, because of very strong winds none of the four lifeboats could be found. Later one boat was washed ashore containing the only two survivors from a crew of over 50. Most of the bodies of the remaining crew, including James McIntosh, were never recovered.

WORLD WAR II: 1939 - 1945

The war of 1939-1945 is known as World War II, because its theatres of war spread across many countries – even more than did WWI. It set the so-called Axis powers – Germany, Italy and Japan – against the Allies – Britain, its Commonwealth and later the USA and Soviet Russia.

This memorial sets the Braemar war deaths in the context of the campaigns in which they took part. But it should be remembered that elsewhere – notably in Russia and the Pacific – there were massive and continuous campaigns not included here.

THE PHONEY WAR AND DUNKIRK (1939 - JUNE 1940)

On 3 September 1939 Britain and France declared war on Germany. The preceding three years had seen mounting tension between Germany and much of Europe including the German 'take over' of Austria and invasion of Czechoslovakia. The final trigger to the declaration of war, however, was the German invasion of Poland.

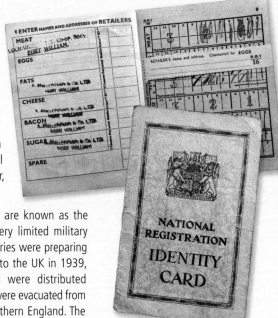

The subsequent months until April 1940 are known as the 'Phoney War' during which there was very limited military engagement in Western Europe. The countries were preparing for war – identity cards were introduced to the UK in 1939, rationing in January 1940, gas masks were distributed throughout the country and some civilians were evacuated from London and later from other parts of Southern England. The British expeditionary force (BEF), as Britain's army was known, took up positions along the French Belgian border, in conjunction with troops from France and the Low Countries.

There was some military action at sea, however, with ships on both sides being attacked and some sunk – the most notable for Britain being the sinking by a German submarine of HMS Royal Oak in Scapa Flow, Orkney on 14 October 1939 with the loss of 835 sailors.

In April 1940, Hitler invaded Norway and Denmark and, in May 1940, he launched the 'Blitzkrieg' (lightning war) invading Belgium, Holland and France. The allied forces were no match for the German army and by mid-June, Belgium, Holland and Northern France had been overrun. In Britain, Winston Churchill, who had become Prime Minister in place of Neville Chamberlain, ordered the BEF to retreat. Thanks to their speed of movement and the bravery of the allied rearguard, around a quarter of a million British troops plus over 100,000 French troops were rescued from the beaches and the channel port of Dunkirk between 26 May and 4 June. Sadly, much of the allied equipment, vehicles, heavy weapons and a large contingent of mainly Scottish troops at St Valery had to be left behind including **Derek McLaren** and **Charles Wright** from Braemar who were Prisoners of War (POWs) for the remainder of the war in Camp Stalag VIIIB in Upper Silesia (now Poland).

THE BATTLE OF BRITAIN (JULY – OCTOBER 1940) & THE BLITZ (SEPT 1940 – MAY 1941)

Britain was now alone against Hitler – and the target of his next invasion plan. For that, Hitler needed to destroy Britain's coastal defences and air force. The period July to September 1940, known as the Battle of Britain, was the first military campaign fought entirely by air forces. Fighting was fierce and the outcome by no means certain. Thanks to the courage, skill and determination of its leaders and pilots, however, the Royal Air Force 'came out on top' forcing Hitler to abandon his invasion plans. During the battle, Braemar suffered its first war fatality – **William John Moir Scott**.

In September 1940, Germany changed tactics and began its campaign of bombing British cities with London being the prime target. The Blitz (as it became known) was intended to destroy Britain's infrastructure and undermine civilian support for the war. The effect, the opposite of Hitler's aim, however, was a strengthening of the determination of the British people to resist and fight back. Britain's cities and civilians nevertheless paid an enormous price during the campaign. German air raids continued more sporadically throughout the war and later, in 1944, became more threatening with attacks by V1 Flying Bombs (Doodlebugs) and V2 missiles.

Myrtle Farquharson

One Braemar casualty of the Blitz was **Myrtle Farquharson**, 15th Laird of Invercauld and Chief of Clan Farquharson. Since early in the war she had been actively supporting the war effort in the London headquarters of the Women's Voluntary Service. Tragically, while visiting an invalid friend on 11 May 1941, she was killed in an air raid on London.

William John Moir Scott (John or 'Scotty') *(Service Number 70611)*

Flying Officer, 41 Squadron of Royal Air Force Volunteer Reserve
Died on 8 September 1940, aged 25
Buried in Dundee Western Cemetery, Compartment 19, Grave 25C

John, born 14 June 1915, was the second of five children and the only son of William Moir Scott and Kathella Campbell of Dundee where the family jute and linen manufacturer, James Scott and Sons, was located.

The family's connection with Braemar dated back to the time of John's maternal grandfather, Dr Alexander Campbell, who initially rented Woodside on Chapel Brae for the summer months and then Sunnyside (subsequently Callater Lodge) on Glenshee Road. During WWII, when their Dundee family home was commandeered by the Fire Service, Kathella (recently widowed) and her daughters moved into Sunnyside, Braemar.

The Scott family loved Braemar and were, for many years, actively involved in the Braemar Royal Highland Society and some of its athletic events. Sports played a major part in John's life. He was an enthusiastic member of the Braemar Golf Club and loved skiing and curling.

John, a very 'bright' boy, won a Mathematical Scholarship from his school, Clifton College, Bristol, and gained a good degree in Engineering from Cambridge University after which he joined the family firm in Dundee. While in Cambridge, he became an RAF cadet and learned to fly – quite unusual in these days.

When he realised war was looming, John volunteered for the RAF, underwent full pilot training, and, at the start of the war, was assigned to 41 Squadron of the RAF Volunteer Reserve as a Spitfire Pilot.

John took part in the 'Battle of Britain' between the RAF and Germany's Airforce (the Luftwaffe). During the first two months of the battle, he survived many 'dog fights' over the English Channel and damaged or shot down several Messerschmitts. The Blitz of Britain's cities began on 7 September. On 8 September, German bombers were spotted crossing the Channel and John's squadron, along with others, were 'scrambled' to intercept them. In the ensuing fracas, John's Spitfire was shot down in flames by a Messerschmitt attacking from behind. From Dover Harbour, John's plane was seen to dive into the Channel. A rescue attempt failed, partly because of the limited search and rescue capabilities at that time but also because of the ferocity of the battle. John was reported to his family as 'Missing'.

It is likely, however, that John managed to bail out of his burning plane as his body was not trapped in the cockpit but washed up at Dover on 1 November, some two months later. He may have been knocked unconscious or died of hypothermia in the cold sea. John's body was returned to Scotland where he is buried in the family grave in Dundee Western Cemetery.

John Scott

Supermarine Spitfire Mark I bearing 41 Squadron's code EB

THE BOMBING OF GERMAN CITIES (1941 ONWARDS)

With most of Western Europe under the control of the Nazis, there was little military activity on the ground there in 1941 or 1942. Instead, early in 1941, Hitler turned his armies east, attacking Greece and Yugoslavia and later Russia, where the Germans, like Napoleon many years earlier, got caught and ground down by the severity of the Russian winter – the first check on the success of the aggressive German army. Three days after Japan attacked the USA fleet in Pearl Harbour on 7 December 1941, bringing the USA into the war in the Pacific, Germany declared war on the USA which had previously been neutral. This brought USA air forces and army into the 'European War' alongside Britain.

As in 1940, Britain's main war activity in Northern Europe over the next two years was in the air. The German Luftwaffe' continued to pound British cities while Britain retaliated with major bombing campaigns over German cities. As well as ruined cities, both sides suffered a major loss of planes and aircrew – two of whom, **Ian McHardy** and **Bob Stewart** came from Braemar.

John Charles Donald McHardy (Ian) *(Service Number 1053447)*

Sergeant, Royal Air Force Volunteer Reserve
Wireless Operator and Air Gunner, 420 Squadron of the Royal Canadian Air Force
Killed in Action on 15 April 1942, aged 25
Buried in Rheinberg War Cemetery, Germany 1. E1

Ian was born at home in Hillview, Chapel Brae, Braemar in July 1916, son of John and Jane McHardy (ms McDonald) and brother of Pauline and Sandy. When Ian was young his father was an estate worker – probably on the Mar Estate. Before his death in 1940, however, John (Senior) had been a greenkeeper (perhaps for either Braemar golf course or one of the Mar Lodge golf courses).

Ian McHardy

At a dance, prior to the start of WWII, Ian had met and subsequently become engaged to Annie (Bunty) Bissett who, along with her parents, lived and worked on Balmoral Estate. Ian and Bunty had great plans for the future.

By April 1942, however, Ian was serving with the Royal Canadian Air Force, 420 Squadron, nicknamed the 'Snowy Owls'. As Wireless Operator and Air Gunner, he was one of the crew of four on a Handley Page Hampden Mark 1 Medium Bomber otherwise known as the 'Flying Suitcase' or the 'Flying Tadpole' because of its cramped crew conditions. The fuselage was only wide enough to seat one person and access was difficult. One report tells of the navigator having to crawl through a tunnel between the pilot's legs in order to get to his station! Seated one behind the other, the crew had almost no room to move and the lack of any heating or toilet facilities only added to the discomfort of long bombing raids.

Described as highly manoeuvrable and a beautiful aeroplane to fly, the Hampden, sadly, was 'undergunned' and proved no match against German fighter planes. During the war, almost half of the Hampdens built were lost on operations. By April 1942, therefore, they were only being used on night missions.

On the evening of 15 April 1942, Ian's plane (AT218 G) was one of seven to set off from Waddington

Handley Page Hampden Mark 1

Airport, Lincolnshire to join another 200 planes on a bombing raid of Dortmund. Having successfully attacked the target and turned for home, AT218 G was shot down close to Neuss, just west of Düsseldorf. There were no survivors. Ian, and the other three crew members are buried in the Rheinberg War Cemetery, some miles north of Düsseldorf.

Robert Charles Stewart (Bob) *(Service Number 1361082)*

Sergeant, Royal Air Force Volunteer Reserve
Navigator, 97 Squadron of the RAF – a Pathfinder Force Unit in 8 Group Bomber Command
Killed in Action on 17 December 1943, aged 21
Buried in Braemar (St Andrew's) Graveyard, Grave 206 (or 74 new numbering)

Bob, son of Charles and Mary Stewart, was born in Braemar in 1922. During WWII it is thought that the family lived in Castleton Terrace, Braemar.

In the early years of the war the success of night bombing raids was seriously limited by the inability of the bombers to navigate sufficiently accurately to destroy individual targets. To overcome this, Bomber Command, in August 1942, set up a special Pathfinder Force (PFF), 97 Squadron, to locate and mark the targets with flares at which the main bombers could then aim. They also tested the latest radio and radar navigational aids for the RAF.

Only volunteers who were highly experienced and prepared to undertake a 50% longer tour of duty than regular bombing crew were accepted into this 'elite force'. Air Vice-Marshal Don Bennett, who pioneered the Pathfinder concept, described them as 'serious, studious, meticulous – and gallant' and their contribution to victory as 'unique'. Because of the nature of the work and the increased number of flights, a PFF crew member's chance of survival was significantly lower than the already poor rate for air crew in WWII. But still men volunteered – including, in November 1943, Bob Stewart and the others in the crew with whom he had flown 23 operational bombing missions as part of the main bombing unit, 207 Squadron.

About two weeks later, on the night of 16 December 1943, a major bombing raid on Berlin was organised, involving 483 aircraft. This was the first action for the new 97 Squadron PFF team of Lancaster Bomber JB219 under the leadership of Flying Officer Kirkwood with Bob Stewart as Navigator. What none of the air crews knew was that Bomber Command had ignored a Met Office recommendation to cancel the raid. Very bad weather was predicted to be affecting East England at the time the bombers would be returning.

The raid completed, the planes turned for home. As they approached the English coast, they hit an extensive blanket of dense fog covering the entire area. Since most planes, including JB219, were by this time very low in fuel they could not 'outfly' the fog. With limited navigational aids and the inability to see any runway, pilots had to make emergency landings and hope they touched down in a field and not in woodland. Sadly,

Memorial plaque at site of crash of JB219
Richard E Flagg / UKAirfields.org.uk

Four of the seven crew of Lancaster Bomber JB219
Bob Stewart second from the left
Pathfinders.com

JB219 in aiming to touch down on farmland crashed into Hayley Wood just south of RAF Gransden Lodge. This was near Bourn, Cambridgeshire where they would have found three runways. The Lancaster burst into flames and the entire crew of seven, including Bob Stewart, were killed. Because of the appalling loss of life and planes, the raid became known as Black Thursday. Worst affected was 97 Squadron with 28 lives lost and 8 aircraft destroyed out of the 21 sent out on the raid.

The bodies of the crew of JB219 were returned to their homes for burial – Bob Stewart to Braemar Graveyard. In September 2007, a memorial plaque was erected on the site of the crash commemorating the seven lives lost.

THE FAR EAST – BURMA AND SINGAPORE (1942 ONWARDS)

While the bombing campaign in Europe continued and intensified, the Japanese moved westwards into Borneo, Java and Sumatra. In December 1941, the Japanese invaded Malaya. Tragically, the Singapore Garrison was inadequately prepared as British High Command completely underestimated the Japanese, thinking that no army could negotiate the thick jungle of the Malaya peninsula. Singapore, with defences designed for a sea-borne attack, was thus unable to withstand the land and air attack which came in February 1942 – even though their forces vastly outnumbered those of the Japanese. The Garrison found themselves trapped within the city, suffering heavy casualties and with no hope of counter-attacking. On 15 February, the Commander of the Garrison, Lieutenant-General Arthur Percival, signed the surrender document and around 80,000 troops became Japanese Prisoners of War (POWs), one of whom was Gunner **James Ferguson** from Braemar. The surrender of Singapore was a great shock and loss to the British. Winston Churchill described it as "the worst disaster and largest capitulation in British history" though he was partly responsible for Singapore being inadequately defended.

James Ferguson *(Service Number 1542871)*

Gunner, Royal Artillery, 6th Battery, 1st Heavy Anti-Aircraft Regiment (or 3rd HAA – there is some confusion in the records)
Died on 10 October 1943, aged 35
Buried in Yokohama War Cemetery, British Sector QA1

James was born in Newbigging Cottage, Glen Cluny, Braemar in June 1908. His parents were James Ferguson, a shepherd on the Invercauld Estate and Ida Ferguson (ms McPherson). By 1937 James was a ghillie living in Chapel Brae Cottage, Braemar. He and Greta Johannah Richard from The Knock, Inverey, married in St Andrew's RC Church, Braemar. When James died in 1943, Greta was living in Ballintuim, Braemar.

In February 1942, James was a Gunner serving with the 1st (or 3rd) Heavy Anti-Aircraft (HAA) Regiment as part of the defence of Singapore. After the surrender to the Japanese, James was initially reported as 'missing' and it was only some considerable time later that he was found to be a POW. He had been taken to the newly

James Ferguson

opened POW Camp, Changi Malai 1, which was the main camp for the captured Singapore British forces. As the Japanese considered surrender to be dishonourable, they treated prisoners appallingly. Many did not survive the harsh forced labour, brutal discipline, punishing climate and lack of food or medicine. Cholera, dysentery and malaria were rife in the camps. All that can be said for Camp Malai 1 was that it was one of the least brutal of the Japanese POW camps.

In early 1943, Japan found themselves short of manpower to keep the 'war machine' running and began shipping POWs to Japan to work in labour camps. James left Singapore on 25 April 1943. For 25 days he travelled on one of the Japanese 'Hellships' – most likely the Kyokko Maru. The conditions on these ships were appalling with the severely overcrowded POWs confined to the hold, subjected to brutal discipline and denied air, light, toilet facilities, adequate food and most importantly sufficient water. Two POWs travelling with James died during the voyage.

On arrival in Japan on 23 May, James was taken to Tokyo 13B Camp at the site of an electro-chemical quarry and cement factory where POWs were sent to work – many in the open-hearth furnaces, chipping out the carbon ingots. The task was hard and boring and the POWs were often forced to work even when quite ill. James survived this life for 4½ months before he died of what was termed cardiac beri beri (heart failure caused by malnutrition) on 10 October 1943. He is buried in the British Sector of Yokohama War Cemetery.

British on way to surrender to Japanese, Singapore 1942
CC-BY-SA

BATTLE OF THE ATLANTIC AND THE CONVOYS: 1939 - 1945

The Battle of the Atlantic was the longest continuous military campaign of WWII. Numerous German submarines (U-boats) roamed the Atlantic, hunting the merchant ships carrying vital food, raw materials, military supplies and troops across the Atlantic, north to Russia and south to the Mediterranean and North Africa.

To protect the supply ships, the Allies used a convoy system. The ships sailed in groups escorted by warships with the capability of spotting U-boats and sinking them with depth charges. RAF Coastal Command anti-submarine aircraft provided additional support for the convoys when they were within flying distance of land. The Germans retaliated, however, by sending several U-boats out together in what became known as 'wolf packs'. They were most effective hunting at night when they could travel on the surface – beyond the range of sonar detection while being hidden from view by the darkness.

It was not until mid-1943 that improvements in mobile radar and the flying distance of anti-submarine aircraft plus increased numbers of escort vessels from the USA, enabled the Allies to gain the advantage over the Germans in the U-boat war and the losses of ships and crew were significantly reduced. In the five years of war, however, the Allies lost more than 3,000 ships and 30,000 crew including **Russell Bell** from Braemar. The Germans, too, suffered heavy losses - over 780 U-boats were sunk and 28,000 crew lost.

John Russell Stewart Bell (Russell)

Acting Sub Lieutenant, Royal Naval Volunteer Reserve (RNVR)
Died on 10 March 1944, aged 20
Commemorated on the Chatham Naval Memorial, Panel 79, Col. 3

Russell Bell

Born in Aberdeen 1923, Russell was the son of William Smith Bell and Ethel Stewart Bell, well known antique dealers with shops on Bridge Street, Aberdeen and Braemar (premises that are now Braemar Gallery) plus a house in Braemar, Collie Bhiethe (opposite the Youth Hostel).

Russell was 'an out-door boy'. During his regular holidays in Braemar, he loved to explore and camp on the surrounding moors. He was also his school's high jump champion. He had a passion for archaeology and a determination to qualify as a GP – with the future hope of combining both, as the GP attached to an archaeological expedition. Russell's strong commitment to 'serving his country' led to him signing up for the Royal Naval Volunteer Reserve (RNVR) immediately he left school – even before telling his family, as he was concerned that his father would not approve!

By 1944, Russell was Acting Sub Lieutenant on the Flower Corvette HMS Asphodel. His former Commanding Officer wrote that he was efficient and very popular with not only his Commanding Officer but also his fellow officers and shipmates.

Corvettes were small convoy escort ships that could be produced quickly, cheaply and in large numbers. They were much slower than other warships and only lightly armed since they were mainly intended for anti-submarine warfare. Crew for the corvettes came mainly from the Royal Navy Reserve and Royal Naval Volunteer Reserve.

Although extremely seaworthy, the Flower Corvettes were reputed to have poor sea-handling ability and given to rolling in heavy seas. As well as the problem of seasickness, men on duty were often drenched with spray while water entered their living quarters when the hatches were opened to access ammunition magazines. Food was mainly tinned or dried and, as the corvettes regularly carried twice as many men as in their original design, some crew were required to sleep on lockers or tabletops. Life on board a corvette, particularly in the Atlantic, was therefore not generally a comfortable experience!

In early March 1944, a convoy with the B4 escort group including HMS Alphodel set off from Liverpool for Gibraltar. To avoid German Bombers operating from Western France, the convoy sailed far to the west, lengthening the voyage to some 15 days. In the very early morning of 10 March, they were attacked in the Bay of Biscay, north west of Cape Finisterre by submarine U-575. HMS Asphodel was torpedoed and sunk

HMS Asphodel (K56)
CC-BY-SA

with only five survivors. Russell Bell was one of the 95 who died. The U-boat was hunted by the other escorts but managed to escape. It was, however, destroyed on 13 March in a joint naval and air attack. Its crew were more fortunate than that of HMS Asphodel as 37 survivors were picked up by Allied ships and only 18 lost.

Russell's body was never recovered. He is commemorated on the Naval Memorial at Chatham.

MEDITERRANEAN THEATRE OF WAR (1940-45) - NORTH AFRICAN CAMPAIGN (1940-43)

The Mediterranean Theatre of War pitched the Axis forces of Italy, Germany and (briefly) Vichy France against Britain, and later American and Free French forces. The Italian Dictator, Mussolini, hoped to create a new 'Roman Empire' around the Mediterranean and displace Britain from its dominance of the Mediterranean and North-East Africa.

Much of the Mediterranean war was fought in the air and sea. The Royal Navy successfully attacked both the Italian and Vichy French navies, and Malta withstood a long aerial siege. Despite the strength of its naval and air forces, Britain did not succeed in preventing Italy and Germany from getting troops and supplies to North Africa.

The land war in North Africa from 1940 to 1943 – the 'Desert War' – was started by Italy seeking to extend its control of territory in North Africa (what is now Libya), and the Horn of Africa (Ethiopia and Somalia). This threatened Britain's control of Egypt and of the sea route through the Suez Canal and the Red Sea.

The initial invasion of Egypt in September 1940 was decisively beaten back by the British and Commonwealth forces. But Italy was then reinforced by the German Afrika Korps under its famous General Rommel – the 'Desert Fox'. Rommel drove the British out of Tunisia and Libya and then attacked Egypt, aiming to reach Cairo and the Suez Canal.

The British 8th Army – including the famous 'Desert Rats' – now commanded by Montgomery, stopped Rommel's advance and then counter-attacked and defeated him at the second Battle of El Alamein in late 1942. This was the first full-scale battle of the war in which British forces defeated a German army and the first battle in North Africa in which the 51st Highland Division took part. The British drove the Germans and Italians back to Tunisia where an American invasion force had overrun Vichy French Algeria and

Army fire 4.5 inch gun, Tunisia, 1943

completed the encirclement of Axis forces from the west. Eventually in May 1943 the last remnants of Axis forces surrendered. This victory made possible the invasion of first Sicily and then Italy by combined Allied forces. One soldier from Braemar who died at the end of the North African campaign was **Charles Mackintosh Grant**.

Captain Alexander Ramsay

Alexander Ramsay (who, in April 1943, became heir to the Fife Estates in Braemar) was a Captain in the Grenadier Guards and fought throughout the North Africa campaign. He was seriously injured in a tank battle in Tunisia in 1943, losing his right leg.

Charles Mackintosh Grant *(Service Number 2881748)*

Private, 5/7th Battalion Gordon Highlanders
Died on 25 September 1943, aged 35
Buried in Medjez-El-Bab War Cemetery, Tunisia (approximately 60 kilometres west of Tunis), Plot 18.B.5

Charles was a son of Charles and Annie Mackintosh Grant and older brother of Willie. He was born in July 1909 in a cottage in Glenfeshie Forest, Alvie (near Aviemore) where his father was a deer stalker. By the outbreak of WWII, young Charles was a gamekeeper on the Mar Estate and, along with his brother, Willie (and probably his widowed father) lived in Thistle Cottage, Inverey. Village memory is that Charles was a crack shot with a shotgun.

In July 1941, while serving with the Gordon Highlanders, Charles married school teacher Annie Pirie Skene in Glenmuick Church, Ballater where Annie lived. It is likely that the couple planned to live in Canada after the war as Annie's address, when Charles died two years later, was Lasqueti in British Columbia.

In June 1942, Charles sailed with the 5/7th Battalion of the Gordon Highlanders from the Clyde to Egypt. They formed part of the 51st Highland Division sent to join the 8th Army facing the Axis powers (Germany and Italy) led by Field Marshal Rommel, the 'Desert Fox'. Their first test was the second Battle of Alamein.

The orders given to the Gordon Highlanders before going into battle were: "Keep Rommel on the run – and keep him guessing." When Allied victory finally came in May 1943, church bells were rung throughout Britain to celebrate the 8th Army's triumph.

Charles, sadly, was not long able to enjoy the triumph. He survived all the dangers and deprivations of the desert campaign only to be struck down by diphtheria which had reached epidemic proportions in 1943. Unfit to sail with the Gordon Highlanders when they left North Africa bound for the Sicily Campaign, Charles was left as a patient in the 103 British General Hospital at a USA airfield at Chateaudun, Algeria. There he died on 25 September 1943.

Gordon Highlanders crossing the border into Tunisia 1943

MEDITERRANEAN THEATRE OF WAR (1940-45) -
SICILIAN AND ITALIAN CAMPAIGN (1943-45)

Following victory in North Africa, the Allies' next targets were to knock Italy out of the war, to protect Allied shipping from air and sea attacks, and to draw German forces away from the Eastern front. The plan was to invade and occupy Sicily first (as its air bases presented the greatest threat to Allied shipping) before invading the Italian mainland. Churchill maintained that Italy was the 'soft underbelly of Europe', failing to learn the lesson of the abortive Dardanelles campaign he had instigated against Germany's ally Turkey in World War I.

The invasion of Sicily in July 1943 was rapidly successful, though at a heavy cost including **John Ewan** from Braemar. The Mussolini regime in Italy quickly fell and an armistice was negotiated with its successor regime in September 1943. The invasion of the mainland, however, proved much slower because of heavy reinforcements and strong resistance by German troops who disarmed and took over from the Royal Italian Army. German troops continued to resist the Allies' northward advance in central then northern Italy until the very end of the European war in May 1945.

John Ewan

John Hutchison Ewan *(Service Number 2880366)*

Private, 5/7th Battalion Gordon Highlanders
Killed in Action on 20 July 1943, aged 23
Buried in Catania War Cemetery, Sicily, Plot III, Row F, Grave 10

John Hutchison Ewan, youngest son of Donald and Janet Ewan (ms Hutchison) and brother to Robert and Donald, was born in Braemar in 1921. His father worked for Invercauld Estate as a stableman and the family lived in an apartment in the stable complex at Invercauld House. By the time John's father, Don, died in 1944 he had retired from stable work and was recorded as a 'caretaker' living at 5 Castleton Terrace, Braemar.

In WWII all three Ewan boys enlisted. Robert and Donald joined the Royal Engineers while John joined the Gordon Highlanders – the 'local regiment'. He served with the 5/7th Battalion of Gordon Highlanders which was part of the 153rd Infantry Brigade of the 51st Highland Division of the 8th Army XXX Corps.

Having survived the gruelling campaign in the deserts of North Africa and seen the surrender of the Axis forces (Germans and Italians), the 51st were shipped across the Mediterranean in July 1943 to invade and capture the island of Sicily. Once landed in the south of the island the plan was for the 8th Army (including the Gordon Highlanders) to move north

Battle of Sferro - by IGM Eadie (1946)
The Gordon Highlanders Museum, Aberdeen

up the east coast of Sicily and for the Americans to advance north westwards before joining up with the 8th Army in the north of the island.

On 10 July the Allied troops arrived in the south of Sicily. Initially, the 8th Army met surprisingly little resistance as the Germans had concentrated their defence further north around the airfields at Gerbini and were well 'dug in' and camouflaged. To overcome the forces at Gerbini, the 8th Army needed to take the nearby town and bridge of Sferro. Careful forward planning was required but, sadly, time was too short for adequate preparation.

After spending a very unpleasant 19 July on an exposed hot hillside overlooking Sferro, the Gordons moved forward to take the bridge. They experienced the fiercest bombardment they had ever endured which continued all the next day. Casualties were high and, according to a Braemar friend who was positioned close by, it was during one of these bursts of heavy gun fire on 20 July that John Ewan was killed 'right beside the bridge'.

On 21 July, after a particularly heavy bombardment, the Allies' tactics changed to one of defending their gains and it was not until 10 days later that the enemy was finally cleared from the Sferro hills. By 17 August, however, the Allies had succeeded in driving the Germans from Sicily.

John was buried alongside many of his fallen comrades in Catania War Cemetery in Sicily.

D-DAY AND THE BATTLE OF NORMANDY (1944)

After almost five long years of war, the Allies were ready to mount an invasion of France. In the weeks preceding the landings, the Allies practised a series of deceptions designed to mislead the Germans as to the date and chosen landing spot. On D-Day, 6 June 1944, the invasion, code-named Operation Overlord,

British Infantry land on D-Day

began with thousands of troops landing on the beaches of Normandy – the USA forces on western beaches and British and other Allies on the beaches further east. The landings were, however, made very difficult by the bad weather which had already delayed the invasion by 24 hours and also reduced the effectiveness of the air and seaborne bombardment aimed at supporting the landings. Although taken by surprise, with the German leaders elsewhere, there were still sufficient German forces plus mined beaches and strategically placed heavy gun emplacements to delay progress inland and to inflict heavy casualties on the Allied forces.

After advancing from the beaches, the next objective for the British and Canadian forces was to capture the city of Caen and its surroundings in order to establish airfields and to clear the route towards the river Seine and Paris. The Germans brought up reinforcements with many heavy tanks and used the countryside (with many dense hedgerows known as "bocage") to delay and counterattack the advance. Caen – in ruins from Allied bombardment – was captured much later than planned at the end of July. Finally, German forces in Normandy were encircled in the Falaise pocket and had to surrender large numbers of troops and most of their equipment.

The two months of the Battle of Normandy saw the most intense fighting, heaviest casualties, and loss of equipment of the war in North-West Europe. The Allied victory was achieved only at great cost and Braemar lost three soldiers during the campaign – **Charles Thom, Andy Lamont** and **Bill Jolly**.

In addition, **Lieutenant Alwyne Compton** (later Captain Alwyne Farquharson, 16th Laird of Invercauld and Chief of Clan Farquharson since the death of Myrtle in the London Blitz of 1941) was awarded the Military Cross for 'gallantry during active operations against the enemy'. Having joined the Royal Scots Greys in Palestine, he served with them through the North African Campaign and the Italian Campaign. Alwyne arrived in Normandy on D-Day+1 and was caught up in the protracted battle for Caen. On 10 July during Operation Jupiter, one of the several attempts to capture Caen, he went forward alone and, under heavy fire, established the cause of the blockage – five German Tiger tanks! Although by this time seriously wounded, he managed to get back to his unit and send a clear message to his commanders on which they were able to act. For 'outstanding devotion to duty' he was awarded the Military Cross. He celebrated his 100th birthday in May 2019.

Lieutenant Alwyne Compton
later Capt. Alwyne Farquharson

Donaldson Charles Thom (Charles) *(Service Number 100726)*

Major and Acting Lieutenant Colonel, 1st Battalion Gordon Highlanders
Died on 19 June 1944, aged 24
Buried in Ranville War Cemetery, Normandy, B. 29.

Charles Thom was born at home in Hazlehead House, Aberdeen in August 1919. He was the younger son of Donaldson Rose Thom, and Jessy Thom (ms Miller). His father was an advocate and, for a number of years previously, had been secretary of the University of Aberdeen. As Charles' father was a keen mountaineer, the family bought Woodhill on the lower slopes of Morrone,

Charles Thom

raemar and were regular visitors. During WWII Jessy, now a widow of many years, lived in Woodhill.

After finishing at Loretto School, Edinburgh, Charles studied at Jesus College, Cambridge with a view to joining the Colonial Administrative Service. This aim was interrupted, however, by the outbreak of the war when, aged 20, Charles enlisted with the Gordon Highlanders. He received his commission in October 1939 and joined the 1st Battalion of the Gordon Highlanders, part of the 51st Highland Division, in France in February 1940. He was wounded early in June 1940 and returned to the UK thus missing, by a few days, the surrender of the 51st Division at St Valery and subsequent incarceration of the soldiers left behind in a German Prisoner of War camp in Poland.

After his wounds had healed, Charles rejoined the 1st Battalion of the Gordon Highlanders and served throughout the North African and Sicilian Campaigns with the reconstituted 51st Division. In January 1944 he received promotion to Major and returned to France in June as part of the D-Day landings.

With the progress of Operation Overlord stalled around Caen, the British and Canadian forces tried to encircle the town to east and west. On 10 June 1944, both 1st and 5/7th Battalions of the Gordon Highlanders advanced to positions east of Caen, across the River Orne into the heavily wooded bocage which gave the Germans ideal cover for defence and ambush. For several days they encountered strenuous counter attacks by elite German Grenadier troops and suffered many casualties from German artillery and snipers. Charles Thom, at this point holding the rank of Acting Lieutenant Colonel, was one of those killed on 19 June in the latter stages of the German counter-offensive in an area called "The Triangle" in Bavant Woods. Sadly, this occurred just before a lull in the fighting because of unusual and unseasonal bad weather.

Charles, along with a number of his comrades, was buried in Ranville War Cemetery, Normandy.

5/7th Gordon Highlanders occupy a defensive position in a hedge in the Bocage, June 1944
The Gordon Highlanders Museum, Aberdeen

Andrew Lamont (Andy) *(Service Number 2880373)*

Lance Corporal, 2nd Battalion Gordon Highlanders
Died on 30 June 1944, aged 21
Buried in Hottot-Les-Bagues War Cemetery, south west of Bayeux,
Normandy, V.A.3.

Andy Lamont

Andy, son of Peter Lamont and Bessie Lamont (ms Sang), was born in Braemar in 1923. He was the eldest of six children – three boys and three girls. His father, who died in 1936, had been a house painter. When Andy was killed in 1944, his widowed mother and family were living in Mostyn Cottage, Braemar.

During WWII, Andy was a Lance Corporal with the 2nd Battalion of the Gordon Highlanders. They were part of the 15th Scottish Infantry Division of the 227th (Highland) Infantry Brigade who landed in France on 20 June 1944 – two weeks after D-Day.

With the continued failure to capture Caen, alternative strategies had to be evolved. Early on 26 June the Allies began a new offensive against Caen, code-named Operation Epsom. The aim was to cross the river Orne to the west of Caen and take the high ground on the southern approaches to Caen, thus outflanking and seizing the city. Among the forces selected for this offensive, many had little combat experience including the 2nd Battalion of Gordon Highlanders.

Continued bad weather during the first few days of Operation Epsom again prevented the RAF from providing the planned preliminary aerial bombing raid on the Germans. Over the next four days, this resulted in Andy and his comrades being subjected to enemy fire from three directions and bombardment from an elite German Panzer Division. The Allies made only very slow progress and sustained very heavy casualties, almost 60% of which were from the 15th Scottish Division and the Gordons. Very sadly, Andy Lamont was one of these casualties.

Piper leading the 15th Scottish, Operation Epsom

Although Operation Epsom failed to capture Caen (which did not fall to the Allies till late July), the offensive proved a strategic success. The Gordons and their fellow units had tied up and seriously damaged many German units. The Germans had lost the initiative and their command structure and deployment were damaged and never fully recovered.

As was the usual pattern, Andy was first buried in a temporary grave and later reburied, along with many of his colleagues, in Hottot-Les-Bagues War Cemetery, south west of Bayeux, Normandy.

William Jolly (Bill) *(Service Number 2875939)*

Private, 5/7th Battalion Gordon Highlanders
Killed in Action on 19 August 1944, aged 29
Buried in St Desir War Cemetery, Normandy (near Lisieux), III. F.10.

Bill, second son of Charles Jolly and of Margaret Clark Jolly (ms Reid), was born in Bridge Street, Ballater in February 1915. His father was at that time a carter having previously been a farm servant on Braehead Farm, Tullich and later recorded as a gamekeeper on the Abergeldie Estate. In June 1938, Bill married Williamina Baird. At that time, he was a quarry labourer living at the Lion's Face, Braemar.

Bill was a Private in the 5/7th Gordon Highlanders who were part of the 153rd Infantry Brigade of the 51st Highland Division. They had landed in France on D-Day on Juno Beach and thereafter had fought in the 6-week costly struggle to capture Caen.

Once south of Caen, the Allies' next target was to encircle the Germans in the Falaise Pocket.

The Battle of the Falaise Pocket began on 12 August 1944 and lasted until 21 August. The fighting was ferocious as Hitler had ordered desperate and unrealistic counter-attacks and refused to countenance a withdrawal of his armies. In the resulting slaughter,

British soldier helps elderly lady, Caen 1944

over 40 German divisions were wiped out plus scores of tanks, guns and other armaments destroyed, leaving a scene of devastation in the French villages and countryside. The cost to the Allies of equipment and lives lost was also very high – one of whom was Bill who was killed towards the end of the engagement on the 19th August. Bill was buried in St Desire War Cemetery, near Lisieux, Normandy.

German surrender after Falaise, August 1944

THE MEDICAL CARE OF WOUNDED

Only brief mention has been made throughout this Memorial of the vast number of forces who were wounded in the conflict. Providing treatment and care for them was a major undertaking. Experience gained during WWI enabled significant improvements to be made in medical care during WWII. Emergency field hospitals and specialist treatment centres were set up closer to all the major war fronts. More sophisticated treatments were available. Medical staff, however, often still risked considerable danger in rescuing and treating the wounded.

In the UK, the Ministry of Health established a centralised state-run Emergency Hospital Service. Numerous hospitals and wards within hospitals were devoted to the care of war victims, including civilian air raid victims. For safety reasons, a number of hospitals were moved from the cities to country areas. The centralised service also took over control of ambulances and staff, one of whom was **Alistair Lamont** from Braemar, a Sergeant in the Royal Army Medical Corps, who died while in service in Southend in 1944.

2nd Duchess of Fife

Braemar had another close connection with the Emergency Hospital Service – **Princess Alexandra, 2nd Duchess of Fife,** frequently referred to as HRH Princess Arthur of Connaught after her marriage to Queen Victoria's grandson, Prince Arthur of Connaught. During WWI Alexandra trained and worked as a nurse in a major London hospital. She continued her nursing career after the war, becoming a highly regarded theatre sister, capable of performing minor operations. For her work, she was awarded the badge of the Royal Red Cross.

At the outbreak of WWII she refused the position of matron of a country hospital in favour of becoming sister-in-charge of the casualty clearing station of a major London hospital. Shortly afterwards she financed and opened the Fife Nursing Home in London where, as matron, she supervised the care of many casualties of war.

Alistair William George Lamont (Service Number 7347565)

Sergeant, Royal Army Medical Corps
Died on 28 June 1944, aged 50
Buried in Braemar (St Andrew's) Cemetery, Grave 64 (138 in new numbering)

Alistair William George Lamont, son of John and Margaret Montgomery Lamont (ms Dow), was born at home in Mealldarroch Cottage, Mar Estate, Inverey in June 1894.

Alistair had a varied career working for many years with the Mar Estate. On his marriage to Edith Littlejohn in 1926, Alistair, like his father and grandfather before him, was recorded as a taxidermist (known locally as a 'stuffer'). In these early years, however, he also worked as sports attendant for The Princess Royal, Duchess of Fife at Mar Lodge.

Shortly after the birth of his daughter Alexandra (Zan), the family moved to London where Alistair undertook general duties for Princess Arthur of Connaught, Duchess of Fife including driving and teaching Scottish

Country Dancing to, among others, the Duchess of York (better known later as Queen Elizabeth, the Queen Mother). He also played the fiddle and when on leave during WWII, enjoyed family music with himself and Zan on fiddles, son Al on mouth organ and Rob, Marg and David on the comb and paper! Alistair's last years in London were spent working for Hendon Borough Council where, using the experience caring for golf courses gained at Mar Lodge, he set out a 9-hole golf course.

Alistair served in both World Wars. During WWI he was a sapper with the Royal Engineers Transport. Their work was vital, providing and maintaining access routes, weapons maintenance and communications. One recently formed and very important unit was the Signal Service which provided communication by a range of means including the new wireless media, telegraph and dispatch riders.

Alistair Lamont WWI

Alistair was assigned to this service and, as the only man in his section who could ride a horse, was chosen to carry messages on horseback to and from areas inaccessible to wheeled traffic. Alistair was wounded in the shoulder or side in 1917 and spent some time in Edmonton Military Hospital in North London.

Edith, and the now five Lamont children, returned to Braemar at the start of WWII and settled firstly into Deeview Cottage, near Inverey and later into Myrtle Cottage, Braemar. Although being older than many recruits, Alistair volunteered for the Royal Army Medical Corps where he served first as a Corporal and then as a Sergeant in the Hospital at Gravesend, Kent which had been requisitioned by the Government for the RAF. It is most likely that he was later moved to the RAF Southend Municipal Hospital at Rochford, Essex as it was there, on 28 June 1944, that he died very suddenly of a gastric haemorrhage. His body was brought back to Braemar and buried with military honours in the village graveyard following a service in St Andrew's Church.

Alistair Lamont WWII

VICTORY IN EUROPE AND THE FAR EAST 1945

The Allies had made clear in the Casablanca declaration of January 1943 that they would settle for nothing short of unconditional surrender of the Axis powers. This was instigated by President Roosevelt and welcomed by Russia which wanted to see Germany completely crushed. It is still debated whether the wars in Europe and in the Far East and Pacific could have been ended earlier by some form of negotiated surrender.

In Europe, having won the Battle of Normandy the Allies pressed on through France, liberating Paris on 25 August 1944 and then Northern France and most of Belgium. The advance to Germany stalled in Northern Belgium and the Netherlands. The Germans defeated an airborne attack on Arnhem and Nijmegen in

September 1944 preventing the intended crossing of the Rhine. Meantime, Allied supply lines from France became overstretched and it took until November to capture the sea lanes to the crucial seaport of Antwerp. In the depths of winter, Germany launched a surprise counter-attack to try and recapture Antwerp (the Battle of the Bulge) which took until January 1945 to finally defeat.

By March 1945 Germany had exhausted its resources on the Western front. The Allies not only crossed the Rhine in force and in several places but rapidly advanced on a broad front across Germany. From the East the Russians captured Berlin at the beginning of May after Hitler committed suicide on 30 April. Surviving German military leaders agreed to unconditional surrender on VE (Victory in Europe) Day – 8 May 1945. The war in Europe was finally over.

In the Far East the struggle was far from over. Japanese land forces were retreating on all fronts but fought desperately to hold back the Americans making their way from island to island ever closer towards mainland Japan. Faced with increasingly suicidal defence by Japanese army units refusing to surrender and kamikaze (suicide) planes, the USA dropped atomic bombs on Hiroshima (6 August) and Nagasaki (8 August). After this, Emperor Hirohito overruled his military commanders and ordered them to "endure the unendurable" and surrender. The formal act of unconditional Japanese surrender on 2 September 1945 marked not just VJ (Victory over Japan) Day but the end of World War II after six horrendous years of conflict.

Scotland celebrates the end of WWII